Drama

Andy Kempe, Chloe Newman, Bev Roblin

Published by Educational Publishers LLP trading as BBC Active, Edinburgh Gate, Harlow, Essex, CM20 2JE, England

BBC logo © BBC 1996. BBC and BBC Active are trademarks of the British Broadcasting Corporation.

First published 2006

The rights of Andy Kempe, Chloe Newman and Bev Roblin as authors of this Work have been asserted by them in accordance with the Copyright, Designs and Patents Act, 1988.

ISBN 0 563 51562 7

Illustrated by Philip Hood

Edexcel coursework portfolio on pp 74 by students from Baylis Court School, Slough

Cover photograph: 'Machinal' by Sophie Treadwell directed by Lib Taylor at the University of Reading

Printed and bound by G. Canale & C., Italy

The Publisher's policy is to use paper manufactured from sustainable forests.

Acknowledgements

The Art Archive p 10 (The Swan); The Art Archive/Army and Navy Club/Eileen Tweedy p 11 (Portrait of Nell Gwynn); BBC/Moviestore Collection p 9 (*Fawlty Towers*); The Bridgeman Art Library/*Farce Actors Dancing* (oil on panel) by Quast, Pieter Jansz (1605–47) p 9 (*Commedia dell'arte* troupe); www.ghostpicturesltd.com/www. nelsonthornes.com p 57 (*Walking with Shadows*); Marilyn Kingwill/ArenaPAL p 48 (*Twelfth Night*); MARY EVANS/EDWIN WALLACE p 8 (Pageant wagon); Moviestore Collection p 25 (*King Lear*); Nils Jorgensen/Rex Features p 51 (*Billy Liar*); RIA Novosti/Lebrecht p 14 (*The Cherry Orchard*); © Robbie Jack Photography pp 16 (*Waiting for Godot*), 21 (*Hay Fever*), 38 (*The Lion King*), 44 (both photographs from *The Crucible*); © Robert Workman/Salisbury Playhouse p 59 (*Be My Baby*); The Ronald Grant Archive p 52 (*Spring and Port Wine*); © RSC/Photography by Keith Pattison/EPO Online p 60 (*As You Like It*); © Simon Annand p 42 (*The Caucasian Chalk Circle*); Tristram Kenton/Lebrecht pp 36 (*Sweeney Todd*), 40 (*Shockheaded Peter*), 47 (*Blue Remembered Hills*), 54 (*A View from the Bridge*)

Every effort has been made to trace copyright holders of material in this book. If, however, any omissions have been made, we would be happy to rectify this. Please contact us at the above address.

D0416554

Contents

About *Bitesize*

GCSE *Bitesize* is a revision service designed to help you achieve success at GCSE. There are books, television programmes and a website, each of which provides a separate resource designed to help you get the best results.

The television programmes are available on video through your school or you can find out transmission times by calling 08700 100 222.

The website can be found at www.bbc.co.uk/schools/gcsebitesize.

About this book

This book is your all-in-one companion for GCSE drama. As with all *Bitesize* guides it is intended to help with your preparations and revision for your GCSE examination. The guide will help you improve your chances of success with practical and written coursework as well as your terminal written examination. It will give you essential background knowledge about different aspects of drama and show you how to use this knowledge to inform and improve your work.

This *Bitesize* book is divided into several sections.

In the first section on drama in different times and places, you will find a brief history of the sort of theatre you are most likely to come across in your GCSE course. This section will help you to make links between your work in drama and that of other playwrights, performers and directors. This section will help you understand how different types of plays have evolved and fit in with major historical events and technological developments.

The medium and elements of drama section gives you essential information about the different ingredients of making, performing and responding to drama. It explains the techniques used by playwrights, actors, designers and technicians to create and stage performances.

In the section on the set texts, the focus on the plays you are likely to study on your GCSE course. The notes put the plays into their historical context, outline the story and help you understand the characters and underlying themes.

The section on the GCSE examinations guides you through the different elements of the drama examinations. The section offers help and advice about preparing for the examination, organising your research and evaluating your work. It also explains how to tackle the tasks and structure your answers to the questions in the written papers.

Examples of successful answers and practice questions are given in the section on questions and answers.

At the end of the book, there is a quick reference section to remind you of key people and terminology that you should be familiar with by the end of your course, advice on avoiding common mistakes, two quick quizzes to test you and a last-minute learner with a summary of the skills, techniques and genres you need to know.

About GCSE drama

THE BARE BONES

➤ GCSE drama involves making, performing and critically evaluating drama you have read, seen and been practically involved in.

➤ You can specialise in particular areas of practical work.

> **STUDY HINT**
>
> Always keep your eyes and ears open for things that you think might make good starting points for dramatic exploration.

Exploring themes and issues

Drama is a way of exploring and gaining new insights into the world of human thought and feeling and communicating these to an audience. Whichever board you are taking your GCSE drama with, you can expect to:

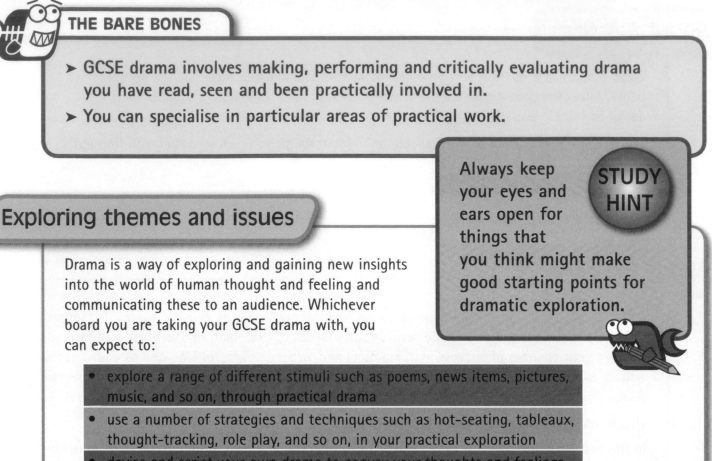

- explore a range of different stimuli such as poems, news items, pictures, music, and so on, through practical drama
- use a number of strategies and techniques such as hot-seating, tableaux, thought-tracking, role play, and so on, in your practical exploration
- devise and script your own drama to convey your thoughts and feelings about the different themes and issues that have emerged from your practical exploration.

Exploring process and product

The play that an audience sees on stage is just the tip of a massive iceberg! Most writers throw away far more than they ever publish, having tried out ideas and realised most don't really work. Designers make sketches, diagrams, pictures and models before finally producing what appears on stage. Actors and directors spend a lot of time work-shopping ideas trying to find the best way to play characters and make scenes 'feel right'. Whichever board you are taking your GCSE drama with, you can expect to:

- explore the different elements that make up a performance, e.g the use of voice, movement and gesture
- learn about the way set and costume design, lighting and sound, and so on, communicate meaning to an audience
- record the way your ideas and knowledge have developed and evaluate your own and other people's work.

> **STUDY HINT**
>
> Take risks, try things out, and be prepared to learn from things that don't work out the first time.

Exploring context and content

GCSE drama tends only to look at a very small part of the wide world of drama and theatre. Even so, you can expect to:

- learn about drama from different times and places
- explore how drama reflects the times in which it was made and first performed and how the way an audience responds to theatre changes depending on when and where they see it
- consider what you think of as effective and important drama and why.

> **STUDY HINT**
> Make notes in your 'working notebook' about how you are linking different ideas, experiences and knowledge together.

Exploring plays

Whichever board you are taking your GCSE drama with, you can expect to:

- explore the storyline, themes and characters of plays written by professional playwrights
- go and see a number of plays and review them
- learn about how plays are made and what is involved in taking them from page to stage.

> **STUDY HINT**
> The more plays you read and go to see the more your understanding and appreciation of drama will grow.

The working notebook

Use a notebook to:

- record what you did in drama sessions and what your thoughts and feelings about the sessions were
- jot down ideas about roles you are developing
- make sketches and diagrams for costume and set design
- keep notes on plays you are studying and performances you have seen
- record what different drama techniques and explorative strategies you have used
- jot down questions raised for you by your work in drama and notes on things you want to find out more about.

Keeping your working notebook up to date will give you lots of material to include in your coursework and write about in your examination.

> **STUDY HINT**
> The 'working notebook' is for you. See it as a personal diary and friend.

THE BARE BONES

➤ Knowing where and when a drama was first created helps you to understand its content and style better.

➤ In an examination, you should show that you understand how dramas you have seen or been involved in relate to the wider world of drama.

Introduction

Most of your work for the GCSE drama examination will concern plays that are written or devised, rehearsed and finally performed in front of an audience in a specially designated space. You should bear in mind that you are working in just one tradition in a much wider world of theatre. In fact, having someone actually write a play that is then performed by actors in a building especially designed for the purpose is very different from many of the forms of theatre that exist around the world today. Many of the writers, directors and designers that you will come across in your GCSE course may themselves have been influenced by theatre from other times and places.

Primitive origins

When: the Stone Age–the present

What happened?

Drama is a way of physically representing experience.

Cave paintings around 7 000 years old depict men dressed as animals re-enacting a hunt. Drama involves people pretending to be someone or something other than themselves (the performers) in front of others who accept the pretence (the audience). Primitive drama is closely related to ritual and ceremony. In some cultures, these rituals have developed into highly sophisticated performances involving dance, storytelling, masks, puppetry and improvised action.

STUDY HINT

Think about common rituals and ceremonies you know that involve people dressing up and behaving in a special way. How do these relate to 'drama' as you understand it?

The Greeks

When: 1200 BCE–500 CE
What happened?

The word drama comes from the Ancient Greek word *dran* meaning 'to do'. Drama was an important part of life for the Ancient Greeks. Plays were staged as part of the festival of Dionysus, the god of wine and fertility. Performances were in open-air **amphitheatres** that could seat up to 20 000 people. Greek plays used a **chorus** to tell and comment on the story. The performers used masks to show what sort of characters they were.

Tragedies drew on stories from Greek mythology, exploring themes such as death, power and justice. **Satyrs** poked fun at these stories and at society. **Comedies** invited the audience to laugh at everyday life.

Key People

Thespis is said to have 'invented' the actor when in one of his productions he had someone step forward and answer the **chorus** and so created the first stage dialogue.

Famous Greek playwrights include **Sophocles** ('Oedipus Rex' and 'Antigone'), **Euripides** ('The Bacchae') and **Aristophanes** ('Lysistrata' and 'The Frogs').

Thespis is remembered in the term 'thespian' meaning 'an actor'.

The Romans

STUDY HINT

Find out which Shakespeare plays re-tell Greek or Roman stories.

When: 250 BCE–500 CE
What happened?

Roman theatre developed what the Greeks had started. The stories were often the same but they were told in a way that appealed to the Roman audience: the **tragedies** became bloodier and the **comedies** became ruder!

The Roman court did not allow the state to be mocked in the way the **satyrs** mocked authority in Greek culture.

Satyrs were replaced by **pantomimes** that featured masked, clown-like dancers.

Key People

Plautus is remembered for his knock-about comedies, such as the 'Menaechmi', which influenced Shakespeare's 'The Comedy of Errors'. **Seneca** developed the five-act format (also used by Shakespeare) for tragedies such as 'Oedipus'.

Medieval theatre

When: 1100–1500
What happened?

After the fall of the Roman Empire, Europe sunk into what is referred to as the **Dark Ages**. The Christian Church was very powerful and it disapproved of the theatre. However, in the 12th century people began to re-enact stories from the Bible. These developed into **Mystery Plays** that were performed on pageant wagons that were taken around the town. Later on, **Morality Plays** such as 'Everyman' appeared to **warn people of the awful things** that would happen to them if they didn't live good Christian lives!

Pageant wagon ▶

Commedia dell'arte

When: 1500–1750
What happened?

Commedia dell'arte began in Italy. It involved highly skilled comic performers improvising stories that mocked **human failings** such as greed, lust and jealousy. The characters were always the same:

Arlecchino – stupid and always hungry (Arlecchino later became better known in England as Harlequin); **Pantalone** – old, lecherous, money-grabbing; **Il Dottore** – always slightly drunk and very boring; **Il Capitano** – a big-headed coward; **Brighella** – usually a shopkeeper who cheats his customers; **Pulchinella** – empty-headed and violent.

Characters such as these can still be seen in modern comedies such as 'Fawlty Towers' and 'Little Britain'.

Rather than using scripts, *Commedia* troupes would work from ideas for scenes (*scenario*) and build in comic devices (*lazzo*) and practical jokes (*burla*).

Key People

Carlo Goldoni (1707–1793) started his career creating scenario for *Commedia* troupes but saw that the actors were losing the skill of improvising new ideas all of the time. He began writing down all of the dialogue he couldn't trust the actors to invent. His plays include 'The Venetian Twins' and 'The Servant of Two Masters'.

STUDY HINT

Think about how Sir Andrew Aguecheek, Sir Toby Belch and Malvolio from 'Twelfth Night' might be seen as *Commedia* characters.

deepen
YOUR THINKING

1 In what ways are the following rituals and festivals related to theatre?

- a traditional wedding
- a 'prom' ball
- a football cup final
- a street carnival

2 Medieval **Mystery Plays** and **Morality Plays** sought to educate people by teaching them Bible stories and **promoting moral values**. To what extent do modern-day dramas try to do this? Do you think they should?

3 The original *Commedia dell'arte* troupes performed their entertainments in the street. What special skills do you think street performers need? To what extent would these skills be useful for any live performance?

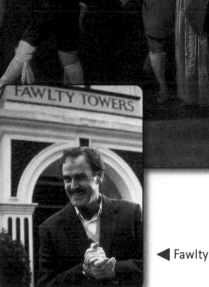

▲ Commedia dell'arte *troupe*

◀ Fawlty Towers

World events

323 BCE
Death of Alexander the Great

218 BCE
Hannibal uses elephants to cross the Alps and invade Italy

54 BCE
Caesar invades Britain

79 CE
Vesuvius erupts and destroys Pompeii

1040 CE
Macbeth murders Duncan and becomes King of Scotland

1066 CE
Normans invade Britain

1400 CE
Death of poet Geoffrey Chaucer

1450 CE
Gutenberg printing press

1492 CE
Columbus lands in the New World

THE BARE BONES

➤ The growth of theatre in the 16th and 17th centuries reflected a new age of scientific discovery and exploration.

➤ As new ideas about the world and human nature emerged, new words and art forms were needed to communicate them.

Elizabethan and Jacobean theatre

When: 1550–1625

What happened?

In 1576, a carpenter and part-time actor called **James Burbage** built 'The Theatre' in London. By 1600, there were at least four other purpose-built, open-air theatres in London. Around one in eight Londoners, including **Queen Elizabeth I** herself, regularly attended performances. Many of **William Shakespeare's** plays reflected the public's fascination with history, foreign places and ideas about everything having its place in the world. When Elizabeth died in 1603 people felt less certain about things. Plays became darker in their themes and the stories more violent. James I came to the throne (the term *Jacobean* is derived from the Latin word for 'James').

> **STUDY HINT**
>
> Research into what new discoveries were made during this period. This will help explain the explosion of new ideas and the growth of language.

The great English poet **Geoffrey Chaucer** (d.1400) had a working vocabulary of 8 000 words. **William Shakespeare** (d.1616) used 24 000 different words.

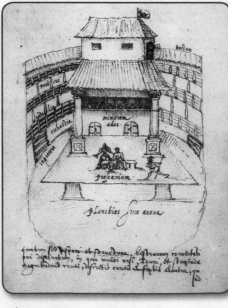

▲ *The Swan*

Key People

William Shakespeare wrote at least 36 plays, most of which are still regularly performed today. Other notable writers and their plays of the period include **Christopher Marlowe** ('The Tragical History of Dr Faust'), **Ben Jonson** ('The Alchemist', 'Volpone'), **John Webster** ('The Duchess of Malfi'), and **John Ford** ('The Broken Heart').

In 1642, Civil War broke out. Playhouses were closed down, partly to stop the spread of plague, partly to stop spies meeting up with each other and partly because the Puritans in government just didn't like the theatre!

The Restoration

What happened?

After the **Civil War** and the execution of Charles I, theatres remained closed until **Charles II** was restored to the English throne. (The period that followed is known as **The Restoration**.) Having lived in France and enjoyed the theatre there, **Charles was keen to re-establish theatre in England**. Many of the plays from this period poke fun at the way rich people behaved.

Women appeared on stage for the first time, notably **Nell Gywnne**, who became the King's mistress.

Key People

William Wycherley's 'The Country Wife' is a comedy about Restoration society's obsession with sex. **Aphra Benn**, Britain's first famous woman playwright, is best known for her sexy comedy 'The Rover'.

Portrait of Nell Gwynn ▶

World events

1400–1600
The Renaissance: massive interest in art, science and medicine; new lands, plants and animals discovered

1564
Birth of Shakespeare

1588
Defeat of the Spanish Armada

1599
The Globe Theatre built

1616
Death of Shakespeare

1620
Pilgrim Fathers settle in America

1642–1651
English Civil War

1660
Charles II restored to throne

1666
The Great Fire of London

1776
American Declaration of Independence

1789
French Revolution

1804
First railway locomotive

1815
Defeat of Napoleon at Battle of Waterloo

1817
First gas lighting in theatres

1829
First typewriter

1836
Samuel Morse patents telegraph

Eighteenth-century theatre

When: 1700–1800

What happened?

Bigger and grander theatres were built in this time. Elaborate scenery was introduced on to the stage. The best actors became the stars of their day. People went to the theatre as much to be seen as to watch the plays – it was 'the place to be'. By the end of the century, some theatres had become so large that the actors had to bellow out their lines and adopt big gestures in order to be heard and understood. Audiences would talk, eat and drink throughout the performances.

Key People

Richard Sheridan wrote a number of brilliant comedies such as 'The Rivals' and 'School for Scandal', while **John Gay** drew on the recently introduced form of opera in his musical play 'The Beggar's Opera'. Well-known actors from this time include **David Garrick**, **John Philip Kemble** and **Sarah Siddons**.

By 1794, **Drury Lane** theatre could hold 3 600 people.

1837
Queen Victoria crowned

1839
First photographs produced

1865
Abolition of slavery in USA

1875
Alexander Graham Bell's telephone

1885
First modern bicycle

1895
First moving picture film show

Victorian melodrama

When: 1800–1900
What happened?

In 1802, **Thomas Holcroft** staged a play called 'A Tale of Mystery'. This launched a craze for plays that offered audiences a mixture of **fast action**, sentimentality and the idea that bad people always get their come-uppance.

> **STUDY HINT**
> A lot of popular films rely on special effects more than on a good story or good acting. Which ones can you think of? In what way are they 'melodramatic'?

In 1800, less than 20% of the population lived in towns, but by 1900, 77% lived in towns. The population of Britain increased from 12 million to over 30 million during this period.

As **the industrial revolution** demanded more workers for the factories, people flocked to the towns from the country. Melodramas provided an **escape** from the noisy and dull routines of industrial life. In order to keep the audiences coming in, theatres had to keep offering new plays. As a result, a lot of the writing was poor and playwrights relied more and more on **stunning special effects** to keep the audience's attention.

Key People

Dion Boucicault wrote exciting plays that had amazing special effects. His play 'The Octoroon' features a Mississippi steamboat exploding on stage. The famous melodramatic image of the heroine being tied to the railway lines and rescued at the last minute originates from **Augustin Daly's** play 'Under the Gaslight' (though in this play it was actually the girl that rescued the fella!) Designers and technicians in Victorian theatres had to be very inventive as they were asked to stage horse races and sea battles as well as finding ever more ingenious ways of making ghosts appear and disappear!

deepen YOUR THINKING

1 Shakespeare's famous character Hamlet says that the purpose of a play is 'to hold, as 'twere, the mirror up to nature.' In what ways do you think the development of theatre in Shakespeare's time reflected what was happening in art, science and world exploration?

2 In 1642 theatres were closed down for a number of reasons. One was that they made convenient places for conspirators to meet and plot. Another was that drama could be dangerous because of the questions the plays raised about society. Do you think drama can be dangerous? Should it be? Do limits and controls sometimes need to be put in place?

3 Imagine that you have recently moved from the country to a big industrial city in Victorian times. You work in a factory for 12 hours every day. Television, radio and film have not been invented yet and there are few places or opportunities to play organised sport. You can read but gas lighting is dim and expensive. In what ways could the local theatre add to your life?

THE BARE BONES

➤ Drama can be performed on stage, television, film and radio.
➤ Drama makes use of technological developments.

Act natural!

Consider the extent to which plays such as 'Blue Remembered Hills' are naturalistic.

When: 1860–the present

What happened?

The term naturalism is used to describe drama that tries to reproduce 'real' life. Whereas melodrama is all about escapism and excitement, naturalism attempts to show life 'as it really is'. The English playwright **Tom Robertson** began experimenting with this style of theatre in the 1860s. His plays were called 'cup and saucer dramas' because he used real food and drink on stage in scenes that were recognisably 'everyday'. An example of a modern naturalistic drama would be 'Eastenders'.

In naturalistic plays, it is as if the audience is watching other people's lives through a window.

Key People

The Russian playwright **Anton Chekhov** and Norwegian **Henrik Ibsen** both wrote plays which presented stories as if they were slices of real life. The great Russian director **Konstantin Stanislavski** worked intensively with his actors to try and get them to portray the emotional truth of the characters they were playing rather than showing themselves off as actors. In Britain, writers such as **Terence Rattigan**, **J. B. Priestley**, **George Bernard Shaw** and **Noel Coward** developed the form through the 20th century until it became seen as the norm.

◄ The Cherry Orchard

The power of politics

When: 1920–the present
What happened?

After the First World War (1914–1918), a German director called **Erwin Piscator** developed a form of theatre that used film, photographs, banners and recorded voices. Piscator wanted to show that **things are the way they are because of politics**. This meant making the audience think about why characters in plays made the decisions they made and why situations were as they were.

Since Piscator, many playwrights, directors and theatre companies have used theatre to show their thoughts and feelings about political issues.

Key People

A close associate of Piscator was **Bertolt Brecht** whose plays 'The Caucasian Chalk Circle' and 'Mother Courage', as well as many others, had a huge influence on other writers and directors such as **Joan Littlewood** and **Augusto Boal**.

> **STUDY HINT**
>
> Think of examples of recent films or television dramas that have tackled political issues.

American realism

When: 1935–1985
What happened?

America quickly became world leaders in cinema after the invention of moving pictures just over 100 years ago. Hollywood, however, tended to be more interested in selling dreams than in exploring difficult issues. In the theatre though, writers such as **Tennessee Williams**, **Arthur Miller** and **Clifford Odets** were proving to be sharp observers of 'real life' and hard-hitting critics of the American dream that everyone can be happy, wealthy and free with plays such as 'A Streetcar Named Desire', 'Death of a Salesman', 'A View from the Bridge' and 'Waiting for Lefty'.

Key People

Director **Lee Strasberg** developed some of Stanislavski's ideas about acting into a technique known as the method. This basically involves an actor adopting **the psychology of the character** they are playing: if you believe you are the person then you'll behave like them!

Actors such as **Dustin Hoffman** were trained in the method and have been successful on stage and screen.

Theatre of the absurd

When: 1945–1960

What happened?

The massive destruction and madness of the Second World War (1939–1945) made a lot of people question the sense of things. The French writer **Albert Camus** concluded that all human existence was absurd. **Theatre of the absurd** is a term used to describe the plays written at this time that reflected the idea that **nothing much makes sense**. A good example is **Samuel Beckett's** 'Waiting for Godot' in which two tramps spend all day waiting for a Mr Godot to turn up and save them from their miserable existence. He never shows up so they must always return the next day to wait again.

The idea that **life is essentially absurd** had a particular influence on **British comedy**. In the 1950s, 'The Goons' was a popular radio show that featured a number of *Commedia dell'arte* type characters in absurd situations. 'The Goons' influenced 'Monty Python's Flying Circus', which first appeared on television at the end of 1969. By portraying the world as being somehow absurd, writers and performers are often able to make a serious point in a comic way.

Key People

In **Eugene Ionesco's** 'Rhinoceros' the inhabitants of a town turn, one by one, into rhinoceroses, while in **N. F. Simpson's** 'One Way Pendulum' a character attempts to train a number of 'speak-your-weight' machines to sing the 'Hallelujah Chorus'.

▲
Waiting for Godot

STUDY HINT

Think of modern plays and television shows that are comic because of the way they show the world as illogical, strange or beyond a simple understanding in some way.

Angry young men (and women)

When: 1956–1970

What happened?

In the 1950s, the director **George Devine** encouraged a number of new, young writers to put their work on at the Royal Court Theatre. One of these was **John Osborne** whose play 'Look Back in Anger' featured a character called Jimmy Porter who angrily criticised middle-class values.

The term angry young men started to be used to describe anyone who hit out at the establishment.

Until 1968, plays could be censored for 'obscene' language or behaviour (such as nudity), or if their content was considered to be politically or religiously controversial. Since censorship in the theatre was abolished, playwrights have been freer to express their opinions and use the theatre to challenge ideas and beliefs.

Key People

Other writers to emerge in the 1950s and 1960s who were critical of the British class system were **Arnold Wesker** ('Roots', 'Chips With Everything'), **John Arden** ('Sargeant Musgrave's Dance', 'Live Like Pigs'), **Edward Bond** ('Saved'), **Shelagh Delaney** ('A Taste of Honey') and **Ann Jellicoe** ('The Knack'). **Joe Orton** ('Loot', 'What the Butler Saw') was a gifted writer of comedies.

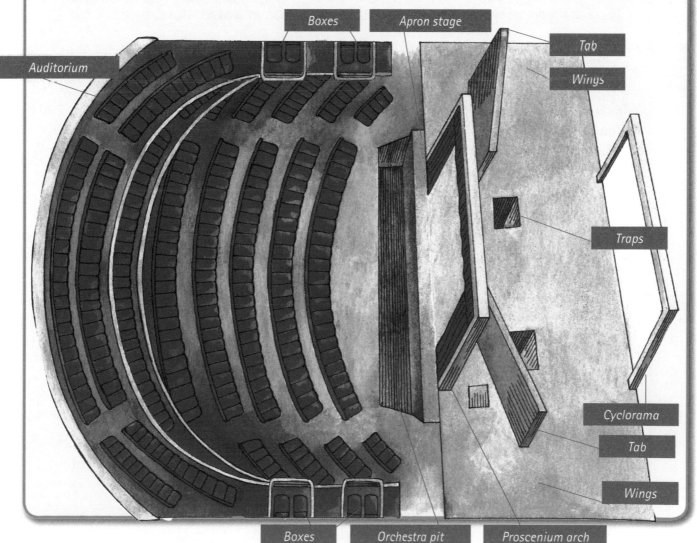

Boxes · Apron stage · Tab · Wings · Auditorium · Traps · Cyclorama · Tab · Wings · Boxes · Orchestra pit · Proscenium arch

THE BARE BONES

➤ More people watch more drama than ever before because of the ready accessibility of television, cinema, video and DVD.

➤ The range of different genres and styles of drama available today is greater than ever before.

➤ There are more people than ever before employed in the creative and broadcasting industries.

STUDY HINT

On programmes such as 'Eastenders', the costumes and sets are realistic and the characters speak in everyday language, but it's not 'real life'. Something interesting has to happen to make a drama worth watching.

Drama in the 21st century

Some people thought that theatre would die out when film became popular at the beginning of the 20th century. The same thing was claimed as more homes got televisions in the 1950s and 1960s. However, the number of people who regularly attend professional theatre in Britain hasn't changed much in the past 100 years (around 2% of the population).

There are more people involved in amateur theatre than in amateur football in the UK.

In 2004, mainstream professional theatre contributed over £2.5 billion to the UK economy.

Theatre cannot compete with film and television when it comes to size of audiences. In 2004, around 21 million seats were sold in professional theatres; compare that with the average audience for each episode of 'Eastenders' of 15 million. However, it's important to remember that 'Eastenders' is also a drama, as are most of the films you are likely to watch.

There is a **healthy relationship between film, television and theatre**. Attendance figures in the theatre rise when plays star actors known for their screen work. Some plays originally written for the theatre become successful films or television dramas ('Closer' by **Patrick Marber**, 'Sleuth' by **Anthony Shaffer**) and vice versa ('Our Day Out' by **Willy Russell**, 'Blue Remembered Hills' by **Denis Potter**, 'Gregory's Girl' by **Bill Forsyth**).

Key People

Major playwrights that have emerged over the last 30 years include **Caryl Churchill** ('Top Girls', 'Cloud Nine'), **Stephen Berkoff** ('Metamorphosis', 'East'), **David Hare** ('Plenty', 'The Permanent Way') and **Sarah Kane** ('Blasted'). Much of the work of these playwrights has been hard-hitting and controversial, and contrasts with the popularity of musicals such as **Andrew Lloyd Webber's** 'Cats' and 'The Phantom of the Opera' or shows built around rock and pop music, such as 'We Will Rock You' or 'Mama Mia'.

Companies such as **DV8, Theatre de Complicite** and **Forced Entertainment** have been influential in introducing exciting physical elements to performance.

World events

1903
First powered flight

1912
The *Titanic* sinks

1914–1918
First World War

1917
Russian Revolution

1936
First television

1937
First electronic computer

1939–1945
Second World War

1959
First microchip

1961
Berlin wall erected separating communist Eastern Europe from Capitalist West
Yuri Gagarin becomes first man in space

1968
Censorship abolished in British theatre

1969
Man lands on the Moon

1973
Mobile 'phone patented

1989
Collapse of Soviet Union

2001
9/11 – terrorists attack World Trade Centre in New York

deepen
YOUR
THINKING

1 While it started in the theatre over 100 years ago, naturalism remains a popular form of drama. It is the form seen in most films and television series. Actual locations and expensive studio sets are used to give the impression of reality.

Watch a soap opera or popular television series carefully. How much like 'real life' are the characters and the situations? What does this tell you about naturalism as a form of drama?

2 What plays or musicals have you seen on film or television that started life in the theatre?

3 In December 2004, Birmingham Repertory Theatre had to close the production of **Amardeep Bassey's** play 'Behzti'. The play had offended some members of the community so much that they rioted and the playwright received death threats.

Should drama be censored if it is likely to cause offense to some people? Who should decide?

Theatre words

THE BARE BONES

➤ The word theatre comes from the Greek *theatron* meaning 'seeing place.'

➤ A number of technical terms are used to describe what goes on in theatres.

➤ You need to know these terms and be able to use them when writing about your own work and performances you have seen.

Theatre terms

Auditorium	the space where the audience sits, or sometimes stands, to watch a performance.
Backcloth / backdrop	a painted cloth that hangs at the back of the stage to give a scenic background. Backcloths are usually used in proscenium arch stages.
Cyclorama	a rigid canvas or plaster wall at the back of the stage. Lighting or projected images can be used on it to give a sense of space or sky.
Drapes	the curtains that hang on each side of a stage to mask the wings.
Flats	a flat piece of painted scenery made by stretching canvas over a wooden frame. Flats can be dropped onto the stage from the flies or moved in from the wings in grooves cut into the stage.
Flies	the space above the stage used to store scenery suspended on ropes so it can be dropped onto the stage.
Front of house	public spaces such as the auditorium and foyer. The term front of house is also used generally to describe all of the administrative jobs in the theatre such as selling tickets and publicising the play.
FX	an abbreviation for sound effects.

An early sound effects machine was invented by John Dennis in 1709 to create the effect of thunder. Mr Dennis was upset though when his idea was used by another company and proclaimed that they had 'stolen his thunder' – a saying still used today.

Rake	some stages are raked so that the back of the stage is higher than the front to help the audience see the action more clearly. The use of a raked stage gives us the terms upstage (that is towards the back) and downstage (closest to the audience). In many theatres, the auditorium is raked so that people sitting at the back can see the stage more easily.

Extra marks are awarded to candidates who use the correct terminology in their exam answers.

STUDY HINT

The saying 'to upstage' someone means to force them to the back so that they are not noticed. When someone takes 'the limelight' it means they have pushed themselves forward so that they are noticed. This saying comes from the theatres of the 18th century when pans of burning quick lime were put at the front of the stage to light the actors.

STUDY HINT

Find out what other sorts of jobs need to be done front of house.

Scenery	this term includes anything, such as painted backdrops, flats and furniture, which helps to give the impression of a location.
Set	the three-dimensional environment in which an actor performs. A set might be a very realistic representation of a living room, a dungeon or a part of a street. Sets can also be more abstract, offering different levels and types of spaces on which to perform.
Sight lines	imagine a series of invisible lines drawn between a member of the audience and any part of the stage. Ideally, every member of the audience ought to be able to see all of the action. Imagining these sight lines helps the actors and director check that they can.
Stage areas	stage areas are defined from the actors' points of view. So, stage left means that part of the stage that is to the left of the actor when they are facing the audience.
Trap	short for trapdoor. There are a number of different types of traps that are used for different effects but most are designed so that actors can appear or disappear very suddenly.
Wardrobe	where the costumes are made and stored.
Wings	the areas at either side of a proscenium arch stage that cannot be seen by the audience. More generally used to describe any area in which the actors wait before entering the performance space.

STUDY HINT

Consider what sort of set would best suit the text you are studying.

▲ Hay Fever

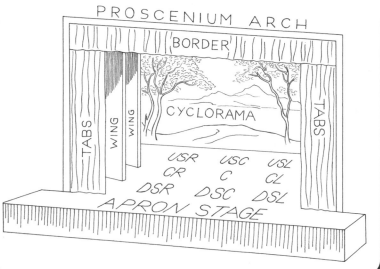

THE BARE BONES

➤ Acting is at the heart of the art form of drama. It involves a person pretending to be another person and physically representing them.

➤ Sometimes actors can represent creatures, objects or even abstract ideas.

The craft of acting

Actors need to have complete control over their voice and body. They understand that even the slightest variation in the way they say or do something can affect the way an audience will interpret their performance. There are two views on how actors deal with this.

One theory is that an actor learns how to tune and play his body as if it were a complex instrument.

Voice	Body
tone	gesture
pitch	facial expression
volume	movement
pace	positioning
accent	posture

STUDY HINT

You need to be able to analyse and describe what acting involves – as well as being able to do it!

In this theory, the actor must remain detached from the character they are playing in order to communicate that character's feelings clearly.

The French writer **Denis Diderot** summed up this idea when he said, 'Actors impress the public, not when they are furious, but when they play fury well.'

Another view of acting is associated with the Russian director **Konstantin Stanislavski**. In this theory, the actor works more from the heart and the head rather than the body by imagining themselves as the character and adopting their psychological and emotional reality.

While different actors may tend to favour one or other extreme, in practice, acting tends to combine both the psychological and physical, depending on the type of drama and the sort of character being played.

Acting terms

Ad lib: this term comes from the Latin phrase *ad libitum*, which means 'as you please'. An ad lib is an improvised comment.

Accepting: this word is usually associated with **improvisations** and refers to the way the improviser readily 'accepts' a fictitious situation.

Aside: an aside is a remark made **directly to the audience** as if the character is letting them in on a secret that the other characters on stage don't know.

Blocking: in **improvisation**, blocking is the opposite of 'accepting'. Blocking also refers to the process of deciding when and how characters should move, sit or stand in different sections (blocks) of a play.

Centring: this is a technique used by actors to find a way of showing a character physically. The idea is to imagine that the character is 'ruled' by a particular part of the body.

Character: it is characters' lines and actions that move the story on and make the points the playwright wants to make.

Characterisation: different actors and directors will interpret the same lines in different ways. Characterisation is **the way an actor decides to use his voice and body to represent the character they are playing.**

Improvisation: improvisation is when **actors make up the words and actions** rather than relying on a script. Some contemporary writers such as **Mike Leigh, Caryl Churchill** and **Ben Myers** have worked closely with groups of actors to develop plays from improvisations.

Pause/silence: when an actor pauses, the audience's attention is drawn to what they have just said and makes them wonder about what will be said next. Pauses give the impression that the characters are thinking which makes them seem more 'real' and creates tension.

STUDY HINT

Think of moments in plays when pauses and silences or the spaces between characters are used to create dramatic effects.

Proxemics: the term used to describe **the way space is being used to communicate meaning.**

Role: the part an actor plays.

Stylisation: naturalism tries to imitate life as it normally appears to be. Stylised theatre, on the other hand, recognises that theatre is an illusion. Stylised characters may, therefore, appear to be **exaggerated** or **unreal**.

deepen YOUR THINKING

1 Choose a scene from a play you are studying. Make notes on how the way characters are positioned on stage in relation to each other (proxemics) could show an audience how they feel about each other.

2 Choose a speech from a play you are studying. Consider where you might place pauses in order to give the speech more dramatic impact or help an audience understand what the character is thinking.

THE BARE BONES

➤ Playscripts are written to be performed, as well as to be read.
➤ Playwrights use a number of techniques that they know will engage a live audience.

Playwriting terms

Antagonist	the character who is in some kind of conflict with the main character or protagonist of the play: the Sheriff of Nottingham is the antagonist to Robin Hood. In many modern plays which explore the complex nature of people and their relationships, it isn't always easy to describe characters as protagonists or antagonists.
Anti-hero	the main character of the play but may not be the sort of person the audience admires.
Chorus	usually, a group of people who are on the edge of the action. They comment on what is going on and sometimes provide links between the events taking place in the play. Sometimes the chorus might be just one person.
Climax/ anti-climax	the climax of the play is the most tense or exciting part. This doesn't mean though that the anti-climax is the most boring bit! Sometimes playwrights deliberately trick an audience into expecting something big to happen and then nothing does. This sort of anti-climax can create a comic effect.
Contrasts	good plays are full of different sorts of contrasts. Heroes seem more heroic if they have a villain to fight; sad scenes can seem more intense if they are contrasted with funny ones.
Dialogue	where two or more people are speaking with each other.
Direct address	when a character talks directly to the audience, such as in an aside. This sometimes involves the character treating the audience as if they are in some way a part of the play. At other times, it involves the actor coming out of role to comment on the play.

STUDY HINT

In writing about plays, you need to show that you understand the different techniques used by playwrights and how they add to the drama in performance.

STUDY HINT

Think of a situation that might appear funny if the audience knows something that a character in a drama does not.

Dramatic irony keeps an audience interested and can be used to create both comedy and tragedy.

Epilogue	it's often used as a way of **summarising** what has happened in the play and giving the audience a few key thoughts to ponder at the end of the play.
Genre	a genre is like a family. Sometimes plays fit easily into one genre, such as tragedy, comedy, history, documentary or thriller, but sometimes they are a mixture and have elements from different families.
Hubris	overconfident pride often accompanied by a lack of humility and resulting in fatal retribution
Metaphor	a way of representing something by drawing a parallel with something else.
Monologue	a speech made by just one character.
Pathetic fallacy	when a human emotion is somehow reflected by a natural occurrence, such as the weather or landscape.

◄ King Lear

Plot	the story of the play is simply the chain of events. Plot refers to the way the story unfolds and how the events are related to each other.
Positioning	where a character is standing or sitting. Playwrights will often use stage directions to indicate when he or she thinks the physical position of a character on stage is of particular importance.
Positioning the audience	the term positioning can also refer to how an audience is encouraged to think or feel about a character or situation.

In J M Barrie's play 'Peter Pan', the audience are asked to clap if they believe in fairies. This is the only way to stop Tinkerbell dying. Sure enough, the audience always claps; they have been *positioned* to do so as they understand that by not clapping the play simply couldn't continue!

Prologue	a speech made to introduce a play. It often reveals just enough of the story so that the audience is intrigued and encouraged to stay and watch the events unfold. A good example is the prologue to 'Romeo and Juliet'.
Soliloquy	a speech made by a character who is thinking out loud as if no one is there to hear them. Perhaps the best-known example of a soliloquy is Hamlet's speech beginning, 'To be, or not to be. That is the question.'

THE BARE BONES

➤ Drama requires a space for performers to be seen by an audience.
➤ Different performance spaces have their own advantages and disadvantages.

Types of performance spaces

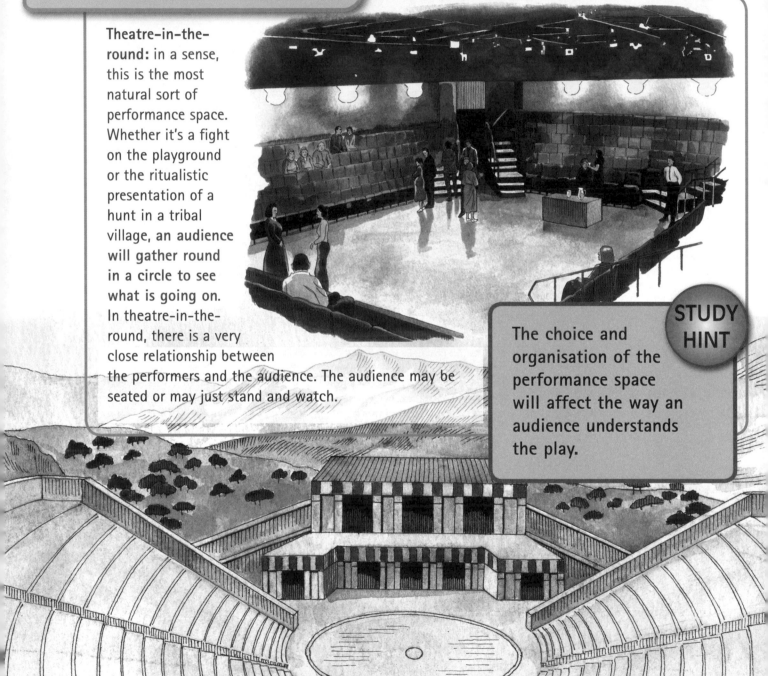

Theatre-in-the-round: in a sense, this is the most natural sort of performance space. Whether it's a fight on the playground or the ritualistic presentation of a hunt in a tribal village, an audience will gather round in a circle to see what is going on. In theatre-in-the-round, there is a very close relationship between the performers and the audience. The audience may be seated or may just stand and watch.

STUDY HINT

The choice and organisation of the performance space will affect the way an audience understands the play.

Amphitheatres	the Ancient Greeks built amphitheatres into hillsides having discovered that sound carried well in naturally formed bowls in the landscape. Some amphitheatres, such as Epidavros, could hold around 20 000 spectators. Amphitheatres allow every member of the audience to see what is going on.
Thrust or open stage	a thrust or open stage is one that juts out from a back wall so that an audience sits or stands on three sides. This sort of stage can give the performers the same sort of close relationship with the audience as theatre-in-the-round, but also allows the back wall to be used to suggest different locations.

STUDY HINT

Theatre involves performers communicating with an audience through the way they speak, move and gesture. An audience has to be able to see what a performer is doing.

Proscenium arch	this was introduced in the 18th Century and is still often thought of as the most traditional type of stage. The effect of the proscenium arch is that the audience gets the impression that they are looking into a picture box, not unlike a television.
Traverse	when a play is staged 'in traverse' the audience sits on either side of a channel. This sort of staging can give an audience the impression of being very close to the action, but it limits the use of scenery.
Promenade	in a promenade performance, the audience does not sit down. Rather, the performers work in different parts of the performance space and the audience moves around to see what is being presented.

STUDY HINT
The use of set, props and lights can also communicate meaning. Different performance spaces can limit the use of these.

deepen

1 What wouldn't you be able to do too much of in a theatre-in-the-round performance?

2 What sort of plays would work well in a proscenium arch theatre?

3 What sort of stage would you like to use for a production of a play that you have been studying? Why?

Drama techniques I

THE BARE BONES

➤ Different drama techniques can be used to explore situations and issues.

➤ They can be used to create characters or investigate how characters think and feel.

➤ Some drama techniques can be used in devising and rehearsing plays.

Introduction

Throughout your GCSE drama course, you will have been using a number of techniques to explore issues, stories and characters in drama. Many of these strategies have their roots in the sort of work professional actors and directors do when they are devising and rehearsing plays. Others have been developed by drama teachers to help students learn about the art form and how to use it in their own work.

When you are writing about your work you need to be able to refer to these techniques in order to explain both what you did and how you developed your ideas and understanding.

Be specific

Just as children in different parts of the country often have their own special names for games they play or sometimes games have the same name but will be played slightly differently. The same is true of drama strategies. When you write about them, you need to make sure that you say a little about what the technique actually involves rather than assuming that the person who reads your work will automatically know what you mean just because you have written the name of the strategy down.

STRATEGY	PURPOSE	ACTIVITY
Conscience alley	To explore what a character might be thinking and feeling at a moment of crisis	Students form two lines facing each other. Someone representing a character in the drama walks slowly along this 'alley'. Each student says what he or she thinks the character might be thinking or feeling at a given moment in the drama.
Cross-cutting	To explore a scene from different perspectives	Cross-cutting means jumping from one moment to another in quick succession. It can involve moving backwards and forwards in time to show how a situation developed and what the consequences were. It can also be used to show how different characters perceived the same situation.

STRATEGY	PURPOSE	ACTIVITY
Essence machine	To represent physically and vocally the key elements of an idea or a situation	Working in small groups, students think of a line and an action linked to a given situation, character or idea. Then, they find a way of linking the lines and actions together so they can be repeated over and over in a mechanical way.
Flashback	To explore the background to a character or a story	Flashbacks can be acted out in different ways. The main point is to provide information about a character's past or something that has happened in the past in order to help explain something about the present situation.
Forum theatre	To explore the different ways a scene might be enacted or how a situation might be resolved	In forum theatre, a small group act out a scene watched by other students who can stop the enactment and offer advice to the actors on either what to do and say next, or how they might have done or said something differently to make it more effective. Sometimes it's useful if the student who stopped the action steps into one of the roles being acted to show what they mean rather than just explain it.
Hot-seating	To explore what a character is like and discover some of the possible reasons as to why they are as they are	One person takes on the role of a character in the drama. The rest of the group ask them questions about what they think and feel or about their lives in general. Sometimes it can be useful to hot seat different characters at the same time by positioning volunteers in different parts of the room. This can show that different characters have different perspectives on a given event or situation.
Imaging	To represent the ideas and feelings that lie beneath the surface of a character or situation	Imaging involves finding a way of showing something physically, and sometimes verbally. Rather than making a tableau like a 3-D photograph, this technique is used to show something that couldn't possibly be photographed, e.g. the idea of love or tension or perhaps what is going on in someone's head and heart at a particular time.

STRATEGY	PURPOSE	ACTIVITY
Narration	To provide either a background to a scene or give further information about a situation that would be difficult or unwieldy to act out	In narration, a performer provides a 'voice-over' to tell a part of a story or comment on a character or a situation. Narration can be a useful device to skip from one part of a story to another, e.g. if a group wanted to condense a fairly long play into just 20 minutes they might use narration to join selected key scenes together.

> **STUDY HINT**
>
> Too much narration can get boring. Audiences prefer to see action rather than hear about it. A narrator needs to be a good storyteller. They must sound interesting and engage each member of the audience as if they are talking to them personally.

STRATEGY	PURPOSE	ACTIVITY
Role play	To explore a situation from the point of view of someone other than yourself	In role play, students imagine that they are someone else in a place somewhere other than the drama. The students don't necessarily have to change the way they speak and move. The main point is to examine people's attitudes and feelings when they are put into some kind of dramatic situation.
Soundscaping	To recreate the sounds and atmosphere of a dramatic situation or moment	Soundscaping involves using the voice and body to capture the different sounds associated with the atmosphere of a place or situation.
Split-screen	To explore different points of view or situations	Split-screen is two scenes showing different perspectives on a given situation, e.g. one scene might show how a group of boys gets ready to go clubbing and the other a group of girls. Split-screen is most effective when one scene freezes while the other activates then switches back again.

> **STUDY HINT**
>
> If you use split-screen or cross-cutting, it is important not to jump too quickly from one thing to another or the audience may just get confused.

STRATEGY	PURPOSE	ACTIVITY
Tableau	To focus on what a particular situation looks like	Tableau is also called freeze-frame or still image. It involves a group of performers adopting a frozen pose as if they had been captured in a photograph. Tableau can be linked to thought-tracking in order to explore what characters are thinking, feeling or saying at a particular moment in the drama. Sometimes parts of a story can be represented through a series of tableaux. The plural of tableau is tableaux; so, one tableau, lots of tableaux.
Thought-tracking	To explore what a character is thinking and feeling at a specific moment in the drama	Thought-tracking is like putting a cartoon thinking bubble over a character's head. The drama is frozen and the character is asked to speak aloud what they are really thinking at a given moment. Of course, this may be very different from what they are saying, so the technique can help in the creation and understanding of believable characters.

deepen YOUR THINKING

Think about the way you have used some of these techniques in your own drama sessions. In the table below, choose three techniques you have used. Give an example of when you used each technique and say how it helped you develop your understanding of a character, situation or performance skill.

Technique	Example	How it helped

THE BARE BONES

➤ Lighting helps the audience see the actors.
➤ It creates mood and atmosphere.

Introduction

Lighting is quite a recent addition to the theatre. Performances from Ancient Greek times (1200 BCE) to Shakespeare's day (1600 CE) were performed in the open air in natural daylight. When indoor theatres were first established, candles were used to provide light. The first use of gaslights in the theatre was in 1817. These lights could be focused and made to shine with different intensity. In 1881, the first electric lights were introduced. These were much safer and more adaptable (and they didn't smell!). Today, a number of different types of electric lanterns are used to produce a huge range of effects.

Types of lanterns (also called lamps)

Profile spot

A profile spot gives a strong, narrow beam of light that can be focused on an area of the stage or an actor. The convex lens in the lantern produces a circular beam but shutters inside the lantern can be used to give the beam straight edges.

The bulbs in household lamps are usually 60 to 100 watts. Most bulbs (also called lamps) used in stage lanterns are either 500 or 1000 watts.

Floodlight

A floodlight doesn't have a lens so it can't be focused. Floodlights give a general wash of light. Sometimes floodlights are put together into a batten which can be used to light the cyclorama or act as a footlight at the front of the stage.

Follow spot

A follow spot is a powerful profile spot set on a stand so that it can be moved from side to side and up and down by an operator. It is the sort of light that would be used to make sure a singer or comedian is always lit but can be used in plays to pick out important characters in key moments.

Lamps and lanterns get hot!
Always use heat resistant gloves when working with lighting.

HEALTH & SAFETY!

Fresnel spot

The lens in a Fresnel spot is cut into a series of concentric grooves. This has the effect of spreading the beam more gently. Fresnels are used to provide a more general sort of covering light across the stage though they can still be focused to allow for different intensity.

Houselights

These are the ordinary lights in the auditorium. There is usually the facility to dim these gradually in order to signal to the audience that the play is about to begin.

Par can

Also called a beam light, the par can throws out a strong circular beam of light. It can't be focused but is useful for providing a strong, very theatrical effect (which is why it is often used at rock concerts!).

Stage lights generate a good deal of heat. Performers need to have some practice working under them in order to get used to this.

Special effects lantern

Special projectors can be used to create effects on stage such as moving clouds, rain, fire or psychedelic patterns.

Stropescope

Strobe lighting flickers to a set rhythm. Strobes can give the impression that the action is being slowed down rather like an old silent movie.

Lighting equipment

Barndoors

These are metal flaps that slot into the front of spotlights and help stop the beam spilling onto areas that do not need to be lit.

Cables

This is the correct term for the wires that connect lanterns to sockets and sockets to the control or dimmer board. Cables have a maximum load-bearing capacity – in other words, they can only carry a certain amount of electrical current before they get too hot and burn out.

Cables should never be coiled when in use as they will get dangerously hot. They should always be coiled and stowed away tidily when not in use though, to avoid the risk of people tripping over them.

HEALTH & SAFETY!

Dimmer (control) board

Dimmer boards allow the operator to **pre-set an effect** while another lighting state is running and **then crossover** by using a control slide. The dimmer board can also **automatically time the** fading of one set of lights and the raising of another as well as just flashing lights.

Modern dimmer boards are computerised so that each effect (LX) can be memorised.

Gel

Gel is also known as cinemoid. A gel is a **thin, coloured plastic sheet** that is placed in a frame and attached to the lantern to tint the light. Different coloured lights are used to highlight the set and costumes, as well as create atmosphere. Some colours suggest certain things, for example, red can symbolise danger or bloodshed. Blue suggests night-time, while greens and purples can seem rather unnatural and spooky.

Shining a certain colour onto a piece of scenery or costume that is the same colour will not produce a good effect! Putting a strong red light onto someone dressed in red will simply make him or her look muddy.

Gobos

Gobos are small metal plates that are inserted into a spotlight behind the lens in order to shape the beam and project a **chosen image** onto the stage or cyclorama.

Gobos and stage lamps are coated with a protective chemical. Touching a gobo or lamps with bare fingers will shorten their working life as the natural acids on human skin burn through the coating.

Irises

An iris is a special **type of shutter** that is inserted into a spotlight behind the lens and is used to make the beam smaller.

Safety chains

Lanterns are clamped onto bars with G-shaped clamps but they must always be chained to the bar with a safety chain.

Lanterns should always be secured with safety chains.

HEALTH & SAFETY!

Lighting terms

Blackout

The term used when all of the stage lights are switched off suddenly. Sometimes the effect will be to fade to black in which case the lights will be more slowly dimmed until there is no light.

Cross-fade

The term used to describe the effect of one or more lights being dimmed while another light or lights are being brought on simultaneously.

Patching

Each lantern is plugged into a socket on the lighting rig. The wires from the sockets lead to another plug that is then 'patched' into a **dimmer rack**. Each socket of the dimmer rack is connected to a channel on the control board.

Preset

A lighting control usually has two rows of slides for each lighting channel. This allows the lighting operator to preset the lights for second scene while the first scene is still running, for example. When the scene changes the lights may be cross-faded or the first state taken to blackout and then the second state brought up.

Rigging

The **grid** that the stage lanterns hang from is called 'the rig'. Rigging is the term used to describe the act of hanging the lanterns in their required positions and focusing them onto the performance area.

State

This is the term used to describe what lights are on at any given time.

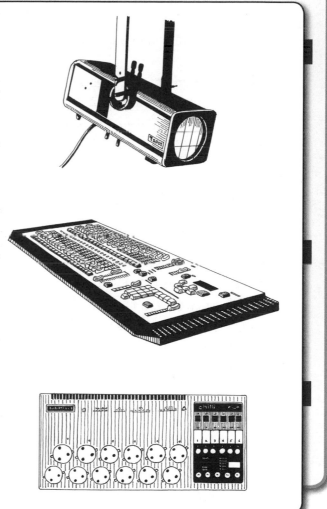

deepen
YOUR THINKING

1 Think about the way different colours affect you. Make a chart like the one below to help you think about where you might use different-coloured gels in a play you have studied and why.

2 Choose two or three pages from a play you have studied which would require a number of lighting changes and annotate them to say what sort of lighting effects you think should be used.

THE BARE BONES

➤ Sound effects add meaning to a production by creating mood, atmosphere, historical period and/or setting.
➤ Sound effects can be live or recorded.

Live sounds

Some sounds occur naturally as a part of a performance, such as the words spoken by the performers, laughter, singing, screaming, or slamming a door.

It may sometimes be necessary to amplify some of these sounds either to ensure that they are heard clearly or to add dramatic effect.

A scream might be deliberately amplified to shock an audience. A snore might be amplified to make them laugh. Laughter might be amplified and put through an echo chamber to make it sound maniacal. Ordinary domestic sounds, such as doorbells or telephones ringing, may need to be recreated on stage to give a sense of reality. These can often be produced live by wiring up real bells rather than using recorded sound. Similarly, radios and televisions used on stage can be fitted with controllable speakers.

Sweeney Todd ▲

The direction a sound effect comes from is important. If a telephone on stage has to ring, then it is no good having a ringing sound coming from speakers placed at the back of the auditorium!

In a group, you could try to generate an atmosphere by recreating the sounds of:
• below decks on an old sailing ship
• an animal-filled jungle
• a scary wood on a wild night
• or a haunted castle.

STUDY HINT

Sound effects can help give a sense of location.
It may be theatrically interesting to have the performers themselves generate a soundscape.

Music

Music can have an immediate and powerful effect on human emotions. It can generate tension, a sense of sorrow or a feeling of fun and is often used to 'underscore' a scene; that is, the music is played in the background but nonetheless adds to the atmosphere.

Introducing a scene with carefully chosen music can place the action of a play in an historical context.

Playing carefully chosen music between scenes can add extra meaning to the action.

STUDY HINT

Think about how music has contributed to the films, television dramas or plays you have seen recently.

Recorded effects

STUDY HINT

The lyrics of songs can add to the dramatic irony of a play. Consider how the choice of songs in 'Be My Baby' does this.

Comprehensive sound libraries are commercially available. These can be very useful for creating background effects, such as weather conditions, traffic or animal sounds, battles and fires.

Pre-recorded effects may need to be edited to the right length to suit your production. The BBC produce an extensive range of sound effects CDs.

deepen YOUR THINKING

1 Go through a script and identify all of the stage directions that suggest that a sound effect is necessary.

2 Think about what the actors are doing. Do any of their actions require sound effects that the playwright has not identified?

3 What ideas do you have for suitable music to open the play or fit in between scenes?

4 Plot the different effects onto a **sound cue sheet** showing the order they come in, when they should come on and at what volume, and how long they should play for (this is called their **duration**).

Costume

THE BARE BONES

➤ Costume includes the clothes and accessories an actor wears to communicate his or her character to an audience.

➤ Costume can influence the way actors feel and move.

Introduction

Costume is a way of **communicating** to an audience the period when the play is set, the age, status, and mood of a character, as well as the style and genre of a play. A costume designer will collaborate closely with the director and set designer to achieve the overall style of a production.

STUDY HINT

Collect old photographs to gain a feel for a particular period.

What can a costume tell an audience?

1 When a play is set

A sense of period is important in some plays. In 'The Crucible', the strict Puritan religion is reflected in the girls' costumes. Their outfits are designed to take away their femininity and to make them conform.

If you are designing a costume that reflects a particular period, remember that it is important to research the era to make sure the design is accurate.

2 Where is a play is set

In some plays, costumes emphasise the geographical location the play is set in. In 'The Royal Hunt of the Sun' by Peter Shaffer, the costumes reflect the play's location in the Andes of the 16th century.

3 About the character

Costume can give an audience information about a character. When Hilda enters in the play 'Spring and Port Wine', the stage direction says: 'She is nineteen... fresh and gay... she wears a bright raincoat and carries *Weekend* magazine.' A designer could build the character's costume from the clues in this description.

The Lion King ▶

Read a play, then make a list of the important points that could influence costume choice.

4 The style or genre of a play

A director may use costume to experiment with the style of a play. Shakespeare's plays are often not performed in Elizabethan style costumes. In 'As You Like It', the costumes in Act 1 might be black and tightly fitting to symbolize the dark, restrictive atmosphere of the court, but when the characters arrive at the forest the costumes might be softer in colour and loose-fitting to show there is more individual freedom.

5 The plot of the play

Costume can be a key factor in the development of the plot sometimes, for example, Rosalind and Viola disguising themselves as boys in 'As You Like It' and 'Twelfth Night' or Malvolio's yellow stockings in 'Twelfth Night'.

Things to remember

- Choice of colour is important. Some colours can look pale and uninteresting under stage lights. Always experiment before you decide.
- Colour can be used symbolically, e.g. black can represent death or a serious character.
- Check the colours and textures of the fabric work with the lights.
- Make sure you are safe and comfortable in a costume. Falling over a dress that is too long can turn a tragedy into a comedy!
- Dress to suit your character, not yourself.
- Check that your costume is suitable for quick changes. A slow costume change can destroy the pace or tension of a play.
- Work as a team – director, set and costume designers and actors – to make sure all your ideas fit together.
- Well-chosen accessories can put the finishing touches to a costume and will show an examiner that you have really thought about your character.
- Try and rehearse in part of your costume. It will help you get into character and you will also discover if it is suitable for the stage, e.g. does it restrict your movement?

A well-designed costume should not draw too much attention, but will enhance your character in his or her given situation.

Finish your costumes well. They can be your friends. They are your enemies if they are badly made and don't hold together.
Director, Ariana Mnouchkine

THE BARE BONES

➤ Make-up is used to 'paint' an actor's face and body in order to change their appearance.

➤ It can be used to create a special character effect, but it is also necessary to counteract the effects of stage lighting.

Make-up through the ages

In the film and television industries, professional make-up artists are employed to prepare actors. In the theatre, most actors apply their own make-up.

The first recorded performer to use stage make-up was **Thespis**, the first actor to step out of the Greek chorus in the 6th century BCE. He used a toxic mix of white lead and red cinnabar!

The introduction of limelight made it necessary for actors to define their faces on stage.

The first 'greasepaint' produced in 1890 was a mixture of zinc white, yellow ochre and lard.

Since the 1940s, changes in stage design and developments in lighting techniques have meant that stage makeup has also had to evolve. Actors now have to take into account how the type and colour of lighting will affect their make-up.

◀ Shockheaded Peter

Different kinds of make-up

1 Straight make-up

This is when an actor enhances his or her own features. It consists of a base foundation, blusher to highlight and shape bone structure, and pencils to emphasise lips and eyes. The amount and type of make-up used will vary according to the age and nature of the character you are playing. Research into period is necessary: a woman in the 1950s would use a different style of make-up to women today.

2 Character make-up

This will include adding additional effects such as:

- nose putty to change the shape of an actor's nose

- flesh wounds, scars, warts, etc.

- crêpe hair for beards and moustaches.

3 Fantasy make-up

Often brightly coloured or containing additional substances, such as glitter, this can be used to create animals or fantasy characters from literature, such as the fairies from 'A Midsummer Night's Dream'. It might also be used to suggest:

- inanimate objects

- emotions and moods

- monsters or aliens.

Fantasy make-up allows you to be as creative as you want.

HEALTH & SAFETY!

Always test for allergic reaction before applying make-up.

deepen YOUR THINKING

Take a look at the following websites.

www.theatrelink.com

www.costumes.org

www.sfpalm.org (San Francisco Performing Arts Library and Museum)

www.cirquedusoleil.com

www.milieux.com

www.makeup-fx.com

The Caucasian Chalk Circle

THE BARE BONES

➤ 'The Caucasian Chalk Circle' is an example of 'epic theatre'.

➤ It aims to make the audience think about the decisions the characters make.

Background

Bertolt Brecht wrote 'The Caucasian Chalk Circle' in 1944 while in exile in America. The rise of the Nazi party in Germany in the 1930s brought with it persecution and oppression. Brecht was in danger because he held Marxist beliefs and was forced to flee his native Germany.

Plot line

The play tells two linked stories, converging them only in the final scene. It is set in Soviet Georgia near the end of the Second World War.

The prologue allows Brecht to get across the moral of the story before the main action begins. It centres on two groups arguing over the ownership of a valley. Before the war, it was owned by goat herders and they argue that this precedence entitles them to own it now. The second group are fruit growers who explain how they can use irrigation techniques to convert 700 acres of infertile land into productive land. A delegate is sent to hear the case and he decides the fruit growers will make best use of the land. Even the goat herders agree! To celebrate this decision the fruit growers put on a play: 'The Caucasian Chalk Circle'.

Both stories begin in a Caucasian city ruled by a governor who is killed by his brother. The Governor's wife flees the city leaving her baby, Michael. Grusha, a kitchen maid engaged to a soldier called Simon, takes the baby, hides him from the Ironshirts and flees. After much danger, Grusha arrives at her brother's house where she is forced into marriage with another man. Simon finds Grusha married to a man she does not love and with a baby. The Ironshirts take Michael away from Grusha and she follows them back to the city.

In the meantime, Azdak has been made a judge after saving the Grand Duke's life. In the final scene, he presides over the trial to decide whether Grusha or the Governor's wife should have the baby. After hearing both sides, he orders Michael to be placed in a chalk circle where both women have to attempt to pull him out to decide the winner. Afraid of hurting the baby Grusha cannot pull him and so reveals herself to be the more deserving of the two women. Azdak gives Michael to Grusha and dissolves Grusha's marriage allowing her to marry Simon.

▲ The Caucasian Chalk Circle

Main characters

Grusha	simple, decent, unsentimental, working-class girl
Azdak	village clerk, appointed judge after saving the Grand Duke's life, a drunk with a strong sense of fairness
Simon	soldier, engaged to Grusha, an honest man
The Governor's Wife	shallow and selfish, has no love for her child, only her estates
The Singer	prime narrator of the stories, provides astute political comment

Major themes

'The Caucasian Chalk Circle' explores the themes of greed, justice, corruption, fairness and social class. Marxist thinking informed Brecht's view of society causing him to rebel against 'justice' that favoured the ruling classes. It explores the notion that resources should go to those who can make best use of them.

STUDY HINT

Look out for clues on staging and meaning in the stage directions that indicate a great deal about character, gesture, detachment, social justice, and so on.

deepen YOUR THINKING

Create a storyboard for the whole play. Try to use just eight frames to tell the whole story – this means you will have to concentrate on what you think are the key moments. Give each frame a title.

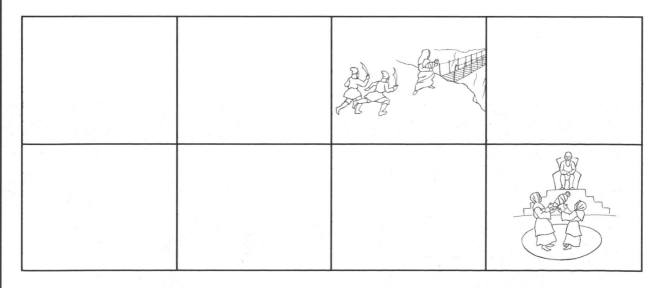

Copy and complete the above storyboard. Compare your version with somebody else's.

THE BARE BONES

➤ Playwright Arthur Miller makes a point about prejudice and injustice in 1950s USA by telling a story set in the 17th century.

➤ When working on 'The Crucible', you need to pay special attention to how Miller makes the audience feel about his characters.

Background

'The Crucible' is based on real events that took place in Salem, Massachusetts in 1692. In the small Puritan town where people's lives were dedicated to the service of God, several teenage girls were caught in the woods dancing round a cauldron. They were accused of engaging in 'the Devil's work'. Some of the girls fell ill and started to suffer hallucinations and seizures. Dancing was forbidden and the girls were terrified of retribution so they looked to shift the blame onto others. It was not long before the residents of Salem began to accuse other villagers of consorting with devils and casting spells. Old grudges and jealousies fuelled the atmosphere of hysteria. The Massachusetts government, heavily influenced by religion, put dozens of people in jail on charges of witchcraft.

A crucible is a container in which metals are heated to extract the 'pure' element from dross or impurities.

Plot line

In Act 1:	some village girls fall ill after being caught dancing in the forest, giving rise to rumours of witchcraft. Reverend Hale arrives and begins his investigations.
In Act 2:	false accusations are made and all those accused are arrested.
In Act 3:	Elizabeth and Proctor are arrested. Hale opposes and quits the court.
In Act 4:	Proctor refuses to confess to witchcraft and to condemn the other accused. He is taken to the gallows.

▲ The Crucible ▲

Main characters

Reverend Samuel Parris	pompous, unpopular and ambitious; talks of 'hellfire' in his sermons
Abigail Williams	a victim, but strong-willed and unscrupulous
John Proctor	the 'hero', decent and courageous, but had an affair with Abigail
Elizabeth Proctor	honest, devout and dignified; keeps to her faith
Reverend John Hale	proud of his knowledge and well meaning, but weak
Tituba	a slave, encouraged by the girls to carry out spells; confesses to anything when terrified
Thomas Putnam	a wealthy but greedy farmer who stands to profit from his neighbours' deaths
Ann Putnam	a bitter woman; seven of her babies died at birth, seeking someone to blame

STUDY HINT

Remember, this is a society in which manners and behaviour are very tightly controlled by custom. The characters' reactions are a response to the cultural inflexibility and religious pressure.

Major themes

'The Crucible' explores the themes of ignorance, fear, lies and revenge. The fear of witchcraft is endemic and based on an ignorant belief in magic, but the *danger* is real enough as the full might of the law is brought to bear on those accused of doing 'the Devil's work'. All the residents of Salem are afraid of being accused of witchcraft, some fear being hanged as a result, some fear the 'powers' of others. Parris fears for his reputation and his position as minister.

Many of the villagers hold powerful grudges against each other and use the pretext of the witchcraft trial to exact revenge on their fellows. Their spite has serious consequences. Abigail wants John Proctor for herself and plots to get rid of Elizabeth. Neighbours use the trial to settle old land disputes. Parris wants to shield himself from enemies he believes are against him.

Lies are told by almost everyone as they try to protect themselves and get revenge on others. The girls lie about their involvement with witchcraft, Proctor lies about his affair with Abigail and all the witchcraft accusations are lies. Finally, there is the 'triumph' of irrationality and superstition over sanity and reason.

deepen YOUR THINKING

1 Make a list of subject-related vocabulary relating to voice, movement, gesture, and facial expressions. Then look at Act 1, from: 'ABIGAIL: Gah! I'd almost forgot how strong you are, John Proctor!' to: 'ABIGAIL: John, pity me, pity me!' How would you play the part of Abigail in this section in terms of voice, movement, gesture and facial expression?

2 Look at the beginning of Act 1. Draw a simple sketch to illustrate in the acting space where you feel characters could be positioned. Give reasons for your choices.

THE BARE BONES

➤ Dennis Potter was a leading writer of television dramas.

➤ On the surface, this play seems quite naturalistic but Potter uses a number of devices to help the audience think about the underlying themes.

Background

Written in 1979, this play is set in the West Country in 1943. The characters are all children (poor, working-class and rural children) but adults play the parts.

Dennis Potter's decision to use adults to play the parts of children did not come from a desire for novelty or humour. He did not want to complicate the audience's reactions with any sentiment or sympathy they might feel at the sight of real children. He felt that real child actors would subtly censor their actions as children naturally do when under adult scrutiny. By using adults, the audience would be able to see and experience the actions and emotions directly.

The children are seen uninhibited by direct influence from grown ups. It is a world of seeming innocence, but the innocence is shattered in a terrible climax.

Plot line

The action takes place during one summer's afternoon in a wood, a field and a barn. It follows seven children, all aged seven, as they play, squabble and fantasise, playing out their fears and hostilities. One character proves particularly vulnerable as the others gang up to taunt him and the play ends in tragedy as he plays his own, dangerous game of pyromania in a barn.

The play takes place in 'real time', with no flashbacks or other theatrical devices to alter time.

Main characters

Willie	easy-going, quite intelligent; uses his brain to counteract Peter's brawn
Peter	strong, inclined to bully, not very bright
Raymond	gentle, stammers, sensitive
John	fair-minded, looks after Raymond, challenges Peter
Angela	pretty, self-centred
Audrey	plain, wants to be Angela's friend
'Donald Duck'	abused by his mother; lonely and frustrated; not liked by the boys but the girls tolerate him and allow him to play with them

Major themes

'Blue Remembered Hills' explores the themes of cruelty, social exclusion and status. It shows how the characters struggle to establish themselves with their peers and how, if they fail, their insecurities can make them miserable and lonely. This pressure to conform and to belong can cause them to behave carelessly and even with cruelty to one another, especially to the weakest.

The play challenges our conceptions of the idyllic nature of childhood, the nostalgic 'blue remembered hills' of our own youth. It shows that childhood can be a fearful place, where emotions are deeply felt and social pressures enormous, especially from other children.

STUDY HINT

The characters are children and children behave differently to adults. Can you remember how you behaved as a seven year old? Note the concentration and level of self-absorption that children exhibit.

STUDY HINT

Think what you did practically when you played a particular scene.

STUDY HINT

The stage directions are as much a part of the play as the dialogue. They are there for a reason. Don't ignore them.

Blue Remembered Hills

deepen YOUR THINKING

1 Select a scene from the play that you have performed or explored practically. Make some notes on the character you played using the following headings: Type of Person, Relationship with Other Characters in the Scene, Voice, Body, Movement, Character's Objectives.

2 Look at the ending of the play, scenes 24 to 29. Write down your ideas on how the burning barn may be portrayed on stage. Pay particular attention to how lighting and sound can be used to create the desired effects.

Twelfth Night

THE BARE BONES

➤ Although this play is essentially a comedy, it also has some dark features.
➤ The play requires an audience to 'suspend its disbelief', that is, to accept that some highly unlikely things happen in the story.

Background

'Twelfth Night' is a comedy written by **William Shakespeare** and was probably first performed on Twelfth Night itself, the 6th of January, in 1602. The Twelfth Night would have been the final night of the Elizabethan Christmas festivities and is the Feast of Epiphany in the Christian calendar. It is a play that revolves around mistaken identity, a common theme in Elizabethan plays.

Plot line

The plot is centred on a love triangle complicated by mistaken identity. Viola and her twin brother Sebastian are separated when they are shipwrecked off the coast of Illyria. Viola disguises herself as a man (Cesario), in order to work at the court of Duke Orsino. Viola falls in love with him. The Duke, meanwhile, is in love with Olivia, a beautiful woman mourning the death of her brother. Olivia falls in love with Cesario (who is really Viola). The plot works itself out in the end as Viola is revealed as a woman and Duke Orsino falls in love with her, and Olivia marries Sebastian, the true masculine equivalent of Viola. There are humourous sub-plots running alongside the main one. Olivia's uncle is the fun loving Sir Toby Belch who encourages his friend, the wealthy but dim Sir Andrew Aguecheek in his affections for Olivia, so that he will stay around and pay for Sir Toby's drinking sessions. Along with Maria, Olivia's sharp-witted servant, he plots a practical joke on Olivia's steward, Malvolio, who is a target in the play because he is a Puritan. The Puritans condemned theatres and other entertainment as corrupting and evil.

◀ Twelfth Night

Main characters

Duke Orsino	rich, sophisticated and handsome; in love with the idea of love
Viola	intelligent, honest, loyal and charming; her only deception is to dress as a man in order to survive
Olivia	beautiful, intelligent and compassionate; capable of self-deception
Sir Toby Belch	Olivia's uncle, irresponsible and carefree, but witty and devoted to the pleasures of the flesh
Malvolio	puritanical, self-important and utterly humourless
Sir Andrew Aguecheek	wealthy, dim and in love with Olivia
Maria	clever, witty and imaginative
Sebastian	brave, handsome and virtuous
Feste	musical and witty clown

Major themes

The play's major themes are love (idealised love, self-delusion and genuine love), deception (including disguise and self-deception) and the festive spirit (pleasure contrasted with Puritanism).

STUDY HINT

Write about what you have experienced practically. Tell the examiner how you would communicate your chosen character to the audience and why. Everything you say must be based upon information given in the text.

deepen YOUR THINKING

1 Create a diagram showing the main characters and their relationships with each other. Remember that many of these are circular relationships.

2 Create a short profile on each main character, covering age, status and appearance. Then select a scene or short section from the play and make notes on one of your chosen character's voice, movement, gestures, facial expressions and how he or she interacts with other characters in that scene or section.

3 Think of the actors you know. Who would you choose to play the part of:

- Duke Orsino
- Viola
- Olivia
- Sir Toby Belch
- Malvolio
- Sir Andrew Aguecheek

Why would you choose them? Why do you think they are suitable?

THE BARE BONES

➤ Keith Waterhouse originally wrote 'Billy Liar' as a novel.

➤ British writers became more interested in the lives of working-class people after the Second World War.

Background

Growing up in a northern industrial town in 1960, Billy Fisher longs to escape from his dull, cliché-ridden life. He invents a fantasy world and dreams of going to London to be a scriptwriter. He is engaged to two girls but is really closer to a third, a free spirit who represents escape. Billy's fantasies and lies catch up with him and he ultimately lacks the courage to break free from his hometown.

Plot line

In Act 1: Billy Fisher, a clerk in an undertakers, lies to his family, telling them he has been offered a job in London as a scriptwriter. He is in trouble at work for stealing post money and for some missing calendars. Billy plans to get back the engagement ring from Barbara, his fiancee, to give to Rita, to whom he is also engaged.

In Act 2: Billy struggles to keep Barbara and Rita apart. His father is not pleased to hear of Billy's engagement to Barbara but attempts to use this as a way into having a meaningful conversation with his son. They begin to communicate but soon fail under a combination of Billy's evasion and his grandmother's single-minded interfering. During the ensuing argument, Florence falls ill and the family get her off to bed. During a stand-up row with Rita, Geoffrey enters with the news of Florence's death.

In Act 3: Billy's boss, Mr Duxbury, comes to arrange the funeral and Geoffrey finds out about Billy's stealing at work, but Duxbury agrees that he will not report Billy to the police if Billy is sensible and pays back what he has taken.

In the front garden, Billy and Liz discuss their plans and dreams and it is clear that they share feelings for adventure, but for Billy they are all in his head. Liz and Billy decide to go to London together that night and agree to meet at the station at 11.00.

Back inside, Billy argues with his father about his plans to work in London and all his bitter feelings about his dull life come to the surface. He packs a suitcase and leaves... but the last thing the audience sees is Billy returning to the silent house, having failed to break away. He cannot leave for a new life in London and returns to his fantasy life at home.

Main characters

Billy Fisher	19 years old, imaginative and creative; wants to escape from his dull background; makes up stories and embellishes his life
Geoffrey Fisher	Billy's father, blustering, hard-working; exasperated by Billy
Alice Fisher	Billy's mother, simple but strong woman; her views on life are set and focused on appearances
Florence Boothroyd	Billy's grandmother, rambles to herself and daydreams; highly critical
Arthur Crabtree	Billy's friend; sympathises with Billy at first but grows impatient with him
Barbara	solid and dull, sees the world through rose-coloured glasses; engaged to Billy
Rita	simple, extrovert and raucous working-class girl; also engaged to Billy
Liz	closest to Billy in character; warm and generous; she transcends the narrow social boundaries that surround her

The practical skills that an actor has at his or her disposal are voice, movement, gesture, facial expression and the use of the space provided.

STUDY HINT

Major themes

The play examines the themes of social conformity and the desire to challenge the existing order. It contrasts the dull and dutiful world of Billy's parents, of Barbara and of Billy's job, where people work hard all their lives for simple rewards, with a volatile and shifting reality that exists in Billy's head, often spilling out into the real world with consequences that are both funny and damaging.

Billy Liar ▶

deepen YOUR THINKING

1 What costumes would you choose for Liz, Rita and Barbara to show the differences in their characters? Give reasons for your choices.

2 Choose a scene you particularly like. Look at the dialogue and find where moments of comedy are used. Annotate the script to show how the humour works and the effect it has.

THE BARE BONES

➤ The play is a simple story about the lives of quite ordinary people.
➤ It shows how even small, quite ordinary things can lead to powerful dramas that change people's lives.

Background

'Spring and Port Wine' was originally written in 1958 but it was not recognised until it was presented in London in 1965.

By 1965, there was greater economic and political freedom, greater religious freedom, and perhaps most importantly, greater individual freedom. The 1960s are remembered as a turning point in British society: a time of opportunity; a time to be young and to express yourself through music, fashion and love. It was also a time of conflict between old and new standards and values. Rafe, the father in the play, is a symbol of the traditional way of life. He reflects the values of an earlier generation.

'Spring and Port Wine' is not only a successful play but an important social document of how life was changing as Britain rebuilt itself after the upheaval of the Second World War. These changes were reflected in British Theatre. By the 1960s, a wealth of new talent, like **Bill Naughton**, started writing about working-class characters and their relationships, using their language and placing them in realistic situations. In many respects, they were the soap operas of the day and were known as 'kitchen-sink dramas'.

> **STUDY HINT**
>
> Throughout the play there are strong hints that Hilda could be pregnant. The audience has to 'read between the lines'. This is an example of subtext.

Plot line

▼ Spring and Port Wine

The play is set in the Compton household in Bolton, Lancashire. Rafe Compton, although a loving father, rules his family with an iron rod. Daisy is the loving mother who acts as a mediator, desperately trying to keep the family happy and together. Two of their children, Hilda and Harold, are starting to question the rigid moral principles Rafe imposes. A trivial incident at teatime threatens to tear the family apart as Hilda angrily decides to leave home for good. The tragic disintegration of the family is avoided by Rafe's self-revelations and the Comptons remain a strong family, who are more open with each other.

Main characters

Rafe Compton	the central character; has great moral and religious principles; loves his family but doesn't always show it; has difficulty accepting that society and his children are changing
Daisy Compton	the traditional mother figure; her job is to stay at home and look after her family; she is torn between her duty to her husband and her love for her children
Florence	the eldest daughter; a teacher, engaged to Arthur; deeply respects her Father, but finds herself torn between her father and her love for her fiancé
Harold	the eldest son; works in the mill; a happy-go-lucky character who is determined to stand up to his father, but somehow he never finds the strength
Hilda	19 years old; full of life; defiant; Rafe's favourite; could be pregnant
Wilfred	18 years old; works in a factory; tries to protect Hilda
Betsy-Jane	the nosy neighbour with a good heart; provides much of the comic relief within the play
Arthur	Florence's fiancé; stands up to Rafe

Major themes

'Spring and Port Wine' explores the themes of family, changing generations and secrets and lies.

Ironically, it is Rafe's insistence on honesty that causes the other members of the family to lie and to keep secrets from each other. When Rafe reveals his secret at the end of the play, the audience is given an insight into what has motivated his behaviour and attitude.

The play is set in the early 1960s during a period of great change, which is reflected in the fashions of the day. Young people felt it was their duty to shock the older generation with their choice of clothes, e.g. mini-skirts! Remember, the key scene is set on a Sunday afternoon when people still traditionally wore their 'Sunday Best'.

STUDY HINT

The style of 'Spring and Port Wine' is naturalistic and well suited to a proscenium arch stage. An important point to remember when setting the scene for the dialogue question in section B of the WJEC written paper.

deepen YOUR THINKING

1 Design a set for 'Spring and Port Wine'. Consider what the set reveals about the characters of Rafe and Daisy. Is a sense of period important? How could the choice of set highlight the themes of family and the changing generations?

2 How would Daisy's costume contrast with Hilda's? Think about the period and consider garments, colour, hair and make-up. Give two reasons for your choices of garments for each character.

3 Select a scene from the play and imagine you are a director giving advice to the actor playing the part of Wilfred. Give the actor advice on character motivation, movement, gesture and facial expressions.

THE BARE BONES

➤ 'A View From the Bridge' is based on a story that Arthur Miller heard when he was working at Brooklyn Harbour about a longshoreman who 'ratted' to the authorities about his cousins who were illegal immigrants.

➤ Eddie Carbone is a tragic hero who contributes to his own downfall.

Background

▼ A View from the Bridge

In a career that spanned more than half a century, **Arthur Miller** became one of America's, and indeed, one of the world's most influential playwrights. Born in 1915 in New York City, both of his parents were immigrants to the United States. Miller continued writing to the end of his life in 2005. His plays are still performed all over the world and he has left theatre a rich legacy.

America has long been seen as the land of opportunity. Between 1880 and 1920, 23 million immigrants entered the country in search of the 'American Dream'. These were mostly Jews, Irish or Italian, like Eddie, Beatrice, Marco and Rodolfo.

But for many of these people, the dream never came true. Immigrants were often reduced to working in poorly paid jobs and living in slums. Ethnic communities grouped together forming large ghettos, thus Eddie's betrayal of the brothers is seen as an unforgivable crime, not only against his family but the whole community.

Plot line

The play is set in a slum area of New York called Red Hook. Eddie Carbone, a longshoreman, his wife, Beatrice, and his niece, Catherine, are an integral part of the community.

From the opening of the play, it is apparent that Eddie is possessive of Catherine. When Beatrice's cousins Marco and Rodolpho, two illegal immigrants, arrive from Italy to look for work, Eddie becomes increasingly uneasy about a developing attraction between Catherine and Rodolpho.

Eddie seeks advice from Alfieri, a lawyer, who warns him to leave things alone. But, in spite of the advice, Eddie rings the immigration authorities and 'shops' the two men. His plan backfires though: Rodolpho's marriage to Catherine will allow him to stay in America, although Marco will be deported.

Intent on revenge, Marco finds Eddie and, in a dramatic climax, kills him in the street. It is left to Alfieri to sum up the tragedy of the situation.

Main characters

Eddie	a simple family man, loved by his family and respected in the community; over-protective towards his niece, Catherine; his relationship with his wife, Beatrice, is beginning to break down
Beatrice	the mediator between Catherine and Eddie; desperate to hold her family together and to steer it away from catastrophe; manages to remain dignified
Catherine	young and vibrant and excited by the prospect of the future; always desperate to please Eddie; she is torn between the two men she loves
Alfieri	not so much a character as a dramatic device; narrates and comments on the action
Marco	a loving husband and father; the strong silent type, who relies on actions to make his point; a dignified man with a strong sense of loyalty towards his family and his community
Rodolfo	full of hopes and ambitions; talks incessantly; genuinely cares for Catherine; she is immediately attracted to him because he is different but he repels Eddie for the same reason

Major themes

'A View From the Bridge' explores the themes of honour, justice, and machismo. It shows how the characters struggle to overcome their flaws and failings as human beings and to fight for what they believe is right and just. It is not coincidental that Miller chooses to have the play narrated by a lawyer. Throughout the play, there is an underlying tension between the law of the land and the code of honour established by the Italian community. The play also challenges the audience's perception of what is 'macho'. It is important to Eddie that he can provide for his family. He constantly feels threatened by what he perceives to be Rodolfo's lack of manliness.

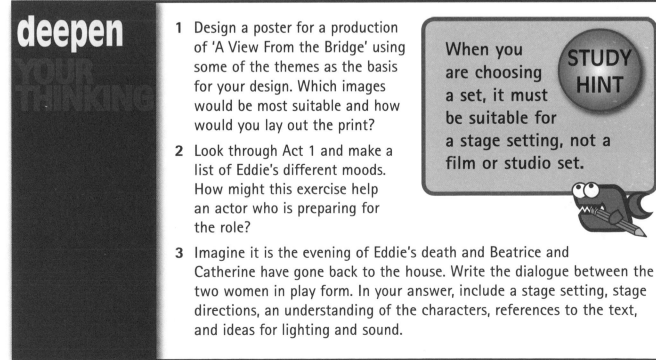

deepen YOUR THINKING

1   Design a poster for a production of 'A View From the Bridge' using some of the themes as the basis for your design. Which images would be most suitable and how would you lay out the print?

2   Look through Act 1 and make a list of Eddie's different moods. How might this exercise help an actor who is preparing for the role?

3   Imagine it is the evening of Eddie's death and Beatrice and Catherine have gone back to the house. Write the dialogue between the two women in play form. In your answer, include a stage setting, stage directions, an understanding of the characters, references to the text, and ideas for lighting and sound.

STUDY HINT

When you are choosing a set, it must be suitable for a stage setting, not a film or studio set.

Walking with Shadows

THE BARE BONES

➤ This play was written for a youth theatre group who helped create and shape the story.

➤ It is a psychological thriller that explores how teenagers think and feel.

Background

Written in 2002, 'Walking with Shadows' is a psychological thriller with a supernatural atmosphere. The playwright, **Ben Myers**, said that his main aim in writing the play was to try and say something about what it is like to be a teenager in today's society. Teenagers face many of the issues dealt with in 'Walking with Shadows': parents divorcing; bullying; eating disorders; self-doubt; and feelings of total isolation. A young audience can easily relate to the language used and the situations encountered in the play.

Plot line

Lorna Moon's life is beset with problems. The only place she can find refuge is in her bedroom, but when she begins to hear voices, she questions whether or not she is going mad or possibly being haunted by the spirit of a young girl.

After she meets Chris, a mysterious and attractive stranger who has suddenly appeared on the scene, the hauntings get more frequent and 'the girl' persuades Lorna to kill herself. Although the attempt fails, the audience finds out that the house has a history of young girls who go mad or try to kill themselves.

Lorna eventually goes into the unknown with Chris, but Jamie, Lorna's younger brother, then becomes the object of the girl's obsession.

Main characters

Lorna Moon	15 years old; struggling to come to terms with the issues in her life
Mr and Mrs Moon	Lorna's mum and dad; wrapped up in their own lives and problems; fail to see the anguish that Lorna is experiencing, until it is too late
Jamie Moon	Lorna's younger brother; fun-loving and mischievous; a typical younger brother
Katie and Sal	typical 15 year olds, who enjoy partying and gossip; good friends to Lorna; try to help her when they become aware things are not quite right in her life
Ricky	another good friend of Sal's; provides some of the contrasting lighter moments

Lucy, Connor and Baz	three characters who make Lorna's life a misery at school; stereotypical bullies; show that Lorna cannot go anywhere to escape her problems
Chris	an enigma; a good-looking boy who all the girls fancy; Lorna confides in him and he tries to protect Lorna but at the end he entices her to go with him; is he a hero or villian?
The Girl	the voice, which becomes the face in the mirror, which becomes the figure in the bedroom; her mission is to destroy Lorna, emotionally, physically and psychologically; pursues Lorna until she achieves her aims
The Shadow Chorus	an effective staging device; they could be the voices in Lorna's head; they could represent unhappy people from the past who also lived in the house
Mr Barness	a next-door neighbour and also a narrator; gives vital information about the history of the house and its occupants

Major themes

'Walking with Shadows' explores the themes of isolation, revenge and failed relationships. Lorna's problems begin when her parents split up and she blames herself for it. This leads to problems in school, isolation from her friends and family, and her physical and psychological problems increase. Lorna's situation allows her to become vulnerable to the mind games of not only the school bullies, but also her own deepest and darkest fears. The play warns us that isolation is never a good thing.

Walking with Shadows ▶

deepen YOUR THINKING

1 As a director, what advice would you give to the actors playing the Shadow Chorus in the opening scene of the play? Think about character motivation, movement and voice. You might also want to experiment with costume, masks and props. In groups, you could rehearse the scene, present it to the rest of the class and discuss the different interpretations. Which one was the most effective and fitted in with the overall style of the play?

2 Look at Lorna's speech at the beginning of Act 2. What advice would you give to an actor playing this role with regard to how she should use her voice? Think about accent, pace, volume and tone. What does this speech tell the audience about Lorna's state of mind?

Be My Baby

➤ The playwright interviewed birth mothers and adopted children about their experiences.
➤ The music from 1964 helps to create atmosphere and gives the play a sense of period.

Background

'Be My Baby' was written in 1997 by **Amanda Whittington**. It is set in 1964 when British society wasn't quite ready for babies born outside of wedlock. Unmarried mothers, their children and families frequently became outcasts. What were the options for an unmarried pregnant girl? Abortion was illegal until 1967 and illegally done abortions often put the mother's life in grave danger. One option for pregnant girls was to go to a home, like St Saviours in the play, where they would be hidden away until the baby was born and given up for adoption.

Plot line

When Mary Adams, 19, finds herself pregnant and unmarried, her mother decides there is only one way to avoid a scandal and allow Mary to have a future. She is taken to St Saviours, a home for unmarried mothers, where she will stay until the baby is born and given up for adoption. At the home, Mary meets three girls, Queenie, Dolores and Norma, all in a similar situation. As the play progresses, Mary realises that, however hard she fights, the baby will be taken from her. Nevertheless, the girls' youthful effervescence shines through and, at the end of the play, the audience believes that for Mary there will be a future after St Saviours.

Main characters

Mrs Adams	Mary's mother; judgemental; thinks herself better than others; desperate to keep up appearances
The Matron of St Saviours	she acts as the voice of reason and the hard face of reality; brisk, highly efficient and has no illusions about the lifestyle unmarried mothers face; cares about the girls but never loses sight that this is her job and never lets emotion affect her judgement; husband was killed after one year of marriage; also keeps up appearances
Mary Adams	a frightened young girl, who develops into a courageous and spirited young woman; believes her baby was conceived in a loving relationship and that her boyfriend will stand by her, if given the opportunity; tries hard to find a way to keep her child; sustained by her records and her friendship with the other girls, particularly Queenie

Queenie	the exact opposite of Mary; loud, cheeky and worldly; not afraid of authority; sees through the illusion the other girls try to create around their situation; has a warm caring side; shows a mature and capable side when she helps Mary deliver the baby
Dolores	she insists she is in a steady relationship; has romantic views about marriage and setting up home; believes she is an 'honest girl'; initially unwilling to face the reality of her situation
Norma	the most tragic of all the girls; her relationship is with a married man; two failed attempts to illegally abort the baby; finds it difficult to come to terms with what she has done; convinced she will be punished by God and is haunted by her baby's cries

Major themes

Truth versus illusion is a key theme. All the girls, particularly Mary, want to face the reality of their situation, but society insists they hide the truth. This theme is linked to another important theme: taking responsibility for your actions. Mary wants to find a job and care for her child, Queenie cared for her first child for nine months until circumstances changed, and even Norma wants to look after her baby once her situation is stable.

Another theme is the importance of friendship. Even in their darkest moments, the girls support and, most importantly, understand each other.

The play is set against a musical backdrop of hits from the 1960s and the romantic and ideal love the girl groups sing about is in direct contrast to the situation the girls find themselves in, but they do give an uplifting soundtrack to a dark tale. The play shows a society that is obsessed with 'keeping up appearances' even at the expense of sacrificing a child's welfare.

Be My Baby ▶

STUDY HINT

When designing a set for the play 'Be My Baby', you need to think about how to suggest the different locations that are on stage at any given time.

deepen YOUR THINKING

1 The title of the play is from a hit record by the 1960s girl group, The Ronettes. Make a list of all the songs in the play, in which scenes they appear, and what effect they have on the mood of that scene.

2 Many playwrights writing in the 1960s were concerned with hypocricy in society. With this in mind, prepare four contrasting freeze frames. Two showing the ordered life of Mary's family (the public) and two showing the chaos Mary's news has brought (the private).

As You Like It

THE BARE BONES

➤ Written in 1600, 'As You Like It' is one of Shakespeare's best-loved romantic comedies.

➤ It contains one of Shakespeare favourite theatrical devices – females disguising themselves as males to avoid detection and to develop the plot.

Background

'As You Like It' was written during the late part of Elizabeth I's reign. During this period England emerged as the leading naval and commercial power in the western world. Just like today, London was a busy centre of culture and high-powered commerce. As a reaction to the stresses of city life, people yearned for what they saw as the simplicity of the countryside where they could relax and 'fleet away the time carelessly'. 'As You Like It' reflects this dream and shows the reality of life in the country and life in the court.

STUDY HINT

When answering a question in the exam, it is useful to quote from the script to illustrate your point.

Plot line

When his brother, Frederick, usurps the good Duke Senior, he flees to the Forest of Arden, where he lives a simple, but idyllic life. His daughter, Rosalind, remains at the palace to be near her friend and cousin, Celia, where she falls in love with Orlando.

▼ As You Like It

Rosalind displeases the new duke, so the two girls flee to the forest disguised as men. Here they meet Orlando who has fled from his cruel brother, Oliver. Rosalind, disguised as Ganymede, suggests they play a game where they woo each other. This allows them to drop all barriers and reveal their true feelings.

When the disguises come off, Rosalind and Orlando realise they are truly in love. There are happy endings for all the other characters too.

Main characters

Rosalind	daughter of the banished duke; tolerated by her uncle; not afraid to stand up for what she believes is right; a passionate character who falls in love at first sight; her disguise allows her to take control and grow into a strong, fulfilled woman
Celia	loyal and unselfish; a strong character who stands up to her father; plans the flight to the forest and supports Rosalind; finds love with the reformed Oliver
Orlando	cruelly treated by his brother and denied his rightful inheritance; a passionate nature; not afraid to show his feelings; physically strong
Jacques	a courtier to the banished duke; a melancholy man with a cynical view of life; remains a solitary figure amongst all the couples, but his idiosyncrasies are accepted
Touchstone	court fool, humorous and good-natured
Oliver	violent, cruel and manipulative; his aim in life is to destroy his brother, Orlando; comes to realise the extent of his brother's love; finds true love with Celia
Duke Frederick	determined to destroy his brother; changes under the influence of the forest; undergoes a religious conversion
Phebe	worships Ganymede (Rosalind); disdainful to Silvius who worships her; has illusions of grandeur; believes she will find someone much better than Silvius; eventually marries him
Audrey	a goatherd; eventually marries Touchstone

During the Elizabethan period, women were not permitted to act or appear on stage. Men would have performed the female roles in Shakespeare's plays. The character of Ganymede would have been played by a man playing a woman playing a man!

Major themes

Friendship and love are pivotal themes in the play. Different experiences of love are examined through the four couples in the forest. Rosalind's and Orlando's love is based on friendship, respect and passion! Celia and Oliver fall in love at first sight. Touchstone's and Audrey's relationship is based on sexual attraction. Silvius and Phebe both experience unrequited love.

The plot of the play revolves around the theme of disguise. Orlando, Rosalind and Celia all use disguises to achieve their goals. The theme of disguise is also explored through the environment of the forest – although it seems idyllic, there are dangers lurking.

Although 'As You Like It' is primarily a romantic comedy, Shakespeare uses the characters of Duke Frederick and Oliver and their relationships with their respective brothers to explore the themes of betrayal and revenge.

deepen YOUR THINKING

1 Create a storyboard for the play. Try and tell the story in eight frames. Give each frame a title that you think sums up the atmosphere or action. For example, Frame one could be entitled 'Brothers at war'.

2 Create two set designs to illustrate the contrasting worlds of the court and the forest. Remember the court is dark and dangerous. The forest is idyllic, but nature can also be wild and dangerous!

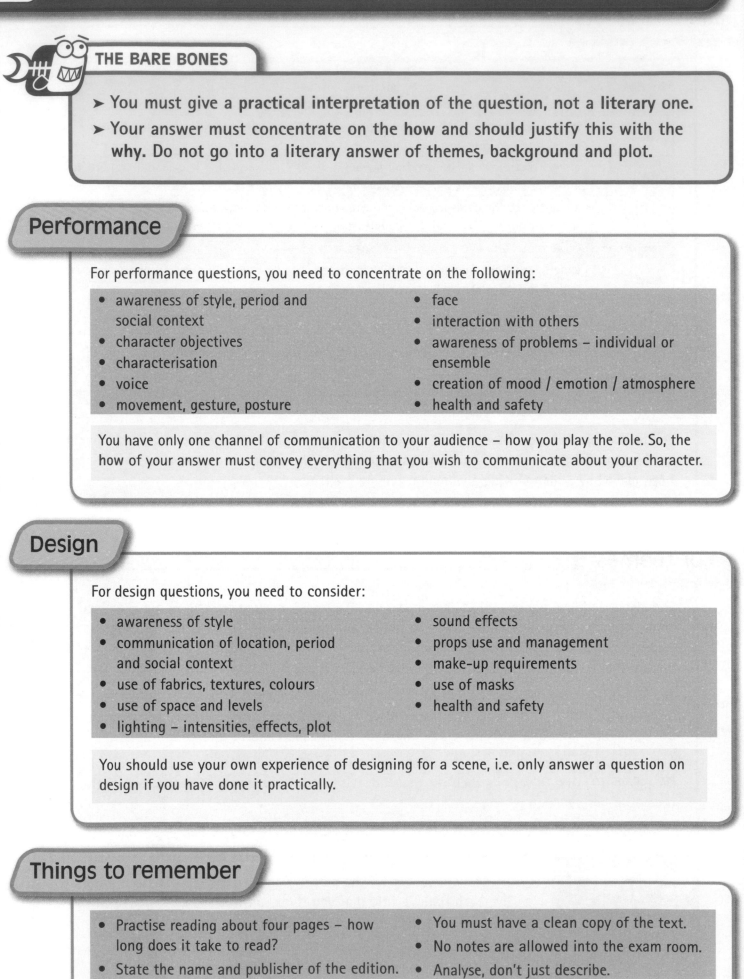

THE BARE BONES

➤ You must give a **practical interpretation** of the question, not a **literary** one.
➤ Your answer must concentrate on the **how** and should justify this with the **why**. Do not go into a literary answer of themes, background and plot.

Performance

For performance questions, you need to concentrate on the following:

- awareness of style, period and social context
- character objectives
- characterisation
- voice
- movement, gesture, posture
- face
- interaction with others
- awareness of problems – individual or ensemble
- creation of mood / emotion / atmosphere
- health and safety

You have only one channel of communication to your audience – how you play the role. So, the how of your answer must convey everything that you wish to communicate about your character.

Design

For design questions, you need to consider:

- awareness of style
- communication of location, period and social context
- use of fabrics, textures, colours
- use of space and levels
- lighting – intensities, effects, plot
- sound effects
- props use and management
- make-up requirements
- use of masks
- health and safety

You should use your own experience of designing for a scene, i.e. only answer a question on design if you have done it practically.

Things to remember

- Practise reading about four pages – how long does it take to read?
- State the name and publisher of the edition.
- You must have a clean copy of the text.
- No notes are allowed into the exam room.
- Analyse, don't just describe.

Writing your essay

Make sure that you understand what the question is asking you to do. Look for key words in the question, e.g. discuss, detail, how.

Ask yourself this key question: where is the information and how do I get it?

The following questions should give you the information you need to write your answer.

- Where is the scene set?
- How does the character enter?
- Why is the character there?
- What is their status?
- What action is there?

- When is it set?
- What is the character doing?
- Who else is present?
- How do they react to each other?
- How do they exit?

Structure your essay and ensure that you don't just describe what you did but why you did it and give evidence from the text to support the points you are making.

A simple essay plan / format

Introduction: Tell the examiner the focus of the answer.

Point: State your idea clearly – in one, two or three sentences.

Justification: Give a reason why you think your point is valid.

Evidence: Support your answer by referring to the text.

Example: Should be the main body of your answer. Demonstrate how your point may be shown on stage through performance / design skills. Cover lots of details and give reasons for your suggestions.

Conclusion: Sum up your main points. Check with the question to ensure you have answered it.

You may make several points, each one being justified and supported by evidence and an example, before writing your conclusion.

Introduction → Point → Justification → Evidence → Example → Conclusion

STUDY HINT

You will answer one or two questions from this section. If you decide to answer two questions, use different plays for each answer.

THE BARE BONES

➤ A good review contains information on what the play is about and how it is performed.

➤ Reviewers should explain why they think and feel as they do about the performance.

Audience and purpose

Reviews of plays adopt a different tone and contain different details about the performance depending on the audience they have been written for.

Here are some reasons people may sometimes read a review.

• They want to know if it is worth going to see.

• They know the play and are interested in how it has been presented on this occasion.

• They are interested in the work of the writer, company or a particular actor.

• They have a personal involvement with the production.

The ideal review to produce for GCSE should contain:

• some essential information about the play itself

• a discussion on how effectively it was presented.

The **audience** for reviews presented as GCSE coursework or examination answers is the examiner. The examiner may not have seen the production you are writing about; they may not even know the play you went to see. However, you should take it for granted that they know a fair bit about theatre and how it works.

The **purpose** of your review is to demonstrate that you can explain why you felt a piece of drama worked in performance or not.

Preparing to write a review

Before going to see the play, make some notes on the following:	
Title	What is the play called? What expectations, if any, does the title set up?
Author	Who wrote it? How does what you know affect your expectations?
Venue	Where will the play be performed? What sort of audience will be present?
Date	Is the time of year or time of day significant in any way?

As soon as possible after seeing the play, jot down some notes on the following:	
Staging	On what sort of stage was the play presented?
Set	What was the set like?
Plot	Summarise the story in as few words as possible.
Themes	What themes were explored in the play?
Genre	Did the play fit into an obvious genre, such as a comedy, tragedy, farce, or murder mystery? Did it have elements of different genres?
Costume / make-up	What did the use of costume and make-up contribute to the drama?
Lighting	How were lights used? Did this add anything special to the performance?
Sound	What different sound effects or music were used to create meaning and atmosphere?
Acting	Could you hear and see all of the actors clearly enough? Did any of them seem better or worse than the others?

Making too many notes during the performance will stop you from getting involved in the play and noticing important details.

STUDY HINT

Marks will be rewarded if you can show a good general knowledge about drama, the different elements that make up a performance and use specialist vocabulary correctly.

STUDY HINT

Structuring a review

In order to write a full and interesting review, you will need to re-order your notes into a piece of engaging continuous prose.

- Give some details of what really struck you about the play itself or the way it was performed.
- Talk about specific aspects of the production that worked well or not.
- Don't be afraid of making your praise and/or criticisms personal to you – just be sure to explain why you feel the way you do.
- Provide a brief conclusion that sums up what you have gained by seeing the production.

deepen

1 Read three different reviews of the same play. Talk about which one:
- gives the most information about the play itself
- tells most about the way the play is performed
- tells most about the personal attitudes of the reviewer!

2 Consider where these reviews come from and what audience they are intended for. To what extent does this explain why they are different?

THE BARE BONES

➤ You need to see at least three or four live productions in preparation for the AQA written exam.

➤ Make detailed notes on some chosen moments.

➤ Questions will ask you to refer to specific scenes or sections of the production you have seen.

About the written exam

On the AQA paper there are four questions in this section.

- One question will be on **performance**, such as: *Discuss, in detail, what you felt to be either the strongest or the weakest performance by one actor and explain the reasons for the strengths and weaknesses. You will need to give details of a particular scene or section.*

- One question will be on **acting** or **design**, such as: *Choose a production you have seen during your course in which the acting or design surprised you. Discuss, in detail, how either the acting or the design contributed to the overall effectiveness of one scene or section and explain in what ways you found it surprising.*

- One question will be on **design**, such as: *Choose a production you have seen during your course in which design played an important part. Discuss, in detail, the strengths and weaknesses of one scene or section. You will need to give reasons to justify your answer. You will need to explain in what ways the design contributed to the production.*

- One question will be on **emotional impact**, such as: *Choose a production you have seen during your course which created a strong audience response. Discuss, in detail, the scene or section that made the strongest impression and explain how the effect on the audience was created.*

Your response will be a personal evaluation of what you have seen.

You must use specific examples from the play to illustrate your points.

You can use your own notes. These must be handwritten or word-processed. They must not be copied or printed from elsewhere, nor can they be notes given to you by the teacher. Reduce your notes to one piece of A4 paper (both sides) per production.

Dramatic techniques

Make brief notes to remind yourself which of these techniques were used in the production:

- narration
- physical theatre
- song
- mime
- chorus

Significant moments

Make brief notes to remind yourself of significant moments in the production. Why were these moments significant? Were they, for example:

- a turning point in the story
- a moment of tension or surprise
- a sad or comic moment
- a moment that communicated character
- a moment that communicated relationships between characters
- a visually striking moment

Tackling questions on performances

Select an actor who impressed you. Jot down notes on the character's age, status and function and decide which performance skills the actor used in the characterisation. Consider the actor's:

- use of voice
- use of body – movement, posture, gesture
- use of face
- interaction with others

In what specific moments in the selected scene or section did the actor impress you and why? What was the reaction of the rest of the audience?

Tackling questions on design

Select a scene where the design impressed you and note reasons why it might have been so effective. Consider:

- style of production
- communication of period and place
- fabrics, textures, colours
- use of space and levels
- use of sound
- use of lighting
- use of management and properties
- use of make-up
- use of masks
- visual impact
- audience reaction

Use sketches and diagrams to illustrate your points.

Sketches and diagrams need to be a decent size so the examiner can see what they are showing. Add annotations to emphasise the important points of what you are trying to show. Putting tiny little drawings down in the corner of the page with no explanation of what they are doing there will be a waste of your time.

THE BARE BONES

➤ All GCSE drama specifications require candidates to read and respond to scripts in some way.

➤ A script is the printed dialogue and stage directions on which a performance is based.

➤ A script needs to be interpreted in different ways in order for it to be performed.

Drama in time and space

Every time you open a particular playscript the words will be exactly the same, just as they are in a novel or a poem. Every time you see a performance of that play though there will always be some differences. This might be to do with you. What you see and hear, and how you understand and feel about that, might be affected by:

• the mood you are in

• where you are sitting (and who with!)

• how many times you have seen or read the play before.

Or it might be to do with the performance. Perhaps the actors speak their lines a little more quickly or one has found a new way of delivering a particular line that has a particular effect. Perhaps the way they use the space or look at each other has changed slightly.

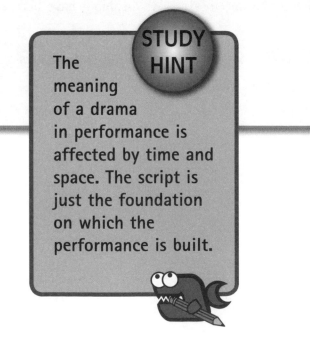

STUDY HINT

The meaning of a drama in performance is affected by time and space. The script is just the foundation on which the performance is built.

STUDY HINT

You need to show an understanding of what actors, directors, designers and technicians have to do to turn a script from words on a page into a performance on stage.

First responses

The first thing to do when you are asked to examine a piece of script is read it! Read every word, including the characters' names and all of the stage directions.

- Make a note of your initial impression.

- Is there a hint of humour, sadness or mystery about the extract?

- Does the extract give you any hint about what the play as a whole might be about?

- Try to imagine the extract being acted out. Where would the characters be in relation to each other? What would the set look like?

Read the extract through again. Annotate it with your ideas about how lines might be spoken and what sort of actions the actors might make.

STUDY HINT

Plays are acted out on stage. They are not 'real life'.

STUDY HINT

Characters' names can sometimes provide clues about what they are like or where they come from.

Who is the playwright addressing?

In performance, an audience will hear the words spoken by actors and see them move about the set. They will also hear any sound effects and see visual effects.

A script may give a number of different people instructions about what must happen on stage, when it must happen and how.

Consider the way the writer of this stage direction demands the attention of a number of different specialists in order to bring it to life:

Set designer

Props

Instruction to actor

Need fake glass

Sound effects

She breaks from him, jumps on the table and seizes the water bottle and smashes it through one of the panes of the window as the train, with a deafening roar, dashes through the station with the whistle shrieking furiously. A cloud of steam billows into the room. JULIA, with a piercing scream, falls from the table and is caught by STERLING.

The train goes on, and – the CURTAIN falls.

The Ghost Train by Arnold Ridley

Can't be real steam – what else could we use?

Use lighting to simulate this?

Instruction to actors

Stage hands

Inspecting the dialogue

When faced with a new script all you have to go on is the language. You need to consider what clues this gives you about:

- when the play is set
- where it is set
- what genre it seems to be
- what the characters are like

- what they feel about the situation they are in
- what they think about each other

Dig beneath the surface. Do not take everything at face value. It may be that there is a sub-text at work:

- When a character says something, do they really mean it? Is there evidence to suggest that they may be joking or hiding the truth?

Watch out for moments of irony.

- Are there moments when the characters are surprised? How is humour or pathos being created?

The dialogue of the play may seem very 'real' but it has been specially crafted to carry meaning and create dramatic effect.

STUDY HINT

It is better to speculate on what seems to be the case rather than state something as fact.

deepen YOUR THINKING

Read this extract carefully.

CHARLES   Nothing of a supernatural nature has happened here.

MISS BOURNE   But it might. Suppose that train should come, what should we do?

CHARLES   What train?

MISS BOURNE   Why, the ghost train that he spoke of.

CHARLES   Oh, that's just a story. *(Going back to barrier)*

MISS BOURNE   But you never know.

TEDDIE *(coming down C)*   I say, if the ghost train comes, I bags we stop it and try and get a lift.

PEGGY   Listen! *(Rising)*

CHARLES   What's up?

PEGGY   Listen! Listen!

deepen
YOUR
THINKING

(They listen)

RICHARD   Well?

PEGGY   I could have sworn I heard a step outside.

RICHARD   A step outside?

TEDDIE *(mimicking him)*   A – step – outside.

(RICHARD goes and looks out of window)

CHARLES   This isn't like you to be jumpy, Pegs.

PEGGY   I'm absolutely certain, Charlie.

TEDDIE   We'll soon settle that. *(Opening the door and going out: then re-entering and clutching at the sides of the door. Horror-struck)*

There's – there's –

PEGGY
                 } Yes? Yes?
ELSIE

TEDDIE *(cheerfully)*   – no one about.

The Ghost Train by Arnold Ridley

Write annotations on this extract in response to these questions.

1   What do the names suggest about the characters and when this play is set? Are there any clues in the style of language about when the play is set?

2   What clues are there about where this scene takes place? What sort of set would you imagine being most appropriate for this scene?

3   Are there any clues about how well different characters know each other? Are there any clues about what the characters think of each other?

4   What expectations are raised at the start of this extract in terms of mood and atmosphere? How does the mood and atmosphere change by the end of the scene?

5   How does Teddie appear to be different from the other characters? What sort of voice do you imagine him having? How might he use facial expressions at different moments and to what effect?

Evaluating devised performance

THE BARE BONES

➤ The WJEC exam requires candidates to evaluate the process that was involved in their practical devising project (Unit 2).

➤ The evaluation should be up to 1500 words in length and is worth 15% of the final mark.

➤ The evaluation should be set out in five sections.

Putting the play into context

Discuss whom you were working with and why you chose to work with them. Give a brief account of the performance and what influenced your decision to choose that particular idea. For example:

Our play is set in the 16th century and involves a girl who is accused of being a witch. She gradually becomes isolated from her friends and family. We chose this idea because I had read 'The Crucible' by Arthur Miller. I thought the tension and atmosphere it created would be effective.

Messages and themes

Discuss the messages, themes and dramatic issues that the group wanted to convey to the audience. Make reference to specific parts of your play and analyse how you tried to make the message clear. For example:

One of the important themes of our play was isolation. We tried to show this in the opening. My character sat alone in the middle of the stage and kept repeating the line 'Why won't they listen?' Gradually, I am surrounded by a group of people who are holding stones. They kept repeating the line, 'Witch child.' As their voices got louder I tried to make myself smaller.

The rehearsal process

Discuss what kind of things you did in rehearsal and how the play developed throughout this process. Why did you decide on a particular acting area? What techniques did you decide to use and why? For example:

While we were rehearsing scene 3 we realised we had not given the audience enough information about the central character's relationship with her mother. We decided that she finds a letter that her mother had written before she died. This gave the scene more emotional impact.

Include a brief description of your character, their motivation, their relationships with other people. Say what you wanted to convey to the audience about the character and how you intended to show this in performance through voice and movement.

Technical aspects

Discuss why you chose the following technical aspects and how they worked in the final performance.

Set design: What kind of environment did you want to create? What problems did you encounter with the set? What worked well? Where did you position objects? Was it successful in the final performance?

Props: Were they symbolic? Were they necessary in the development of the plot? What did the audience learn about a character from individual props?

Lighting: How was lighting used to create mood, atmosphere, location, etc.?

Music and sound effects: Why was a particular piece of music used? What effect did it create?

Costume, hair and make-up: Did your costume show the period your play was set? What did you wear? What colour and fabric did you choose? What did the audience learn about character and the style of the play from your costume choice?

Include visual evidence in this section, e.g. set and costume designs, photographs. Make sure you give each illustration a title or caption so that it is clear what the picture is actually of. Annotations should be used to highlight important aspects of the illustrations.

Evaluating the final performance

Avoid saying things such as, 'I was very nervous but it went well and I didn't forget my lines.'

Break your evaluation down into sections.

Your individual performance: Discuss your use of voice and movement, how you used space, and how you handled props. What scenes did you perform well and why? Where could you have improved? How did the audience respond to your character?

The group performance: Which scenes were effective from a group point of view? How did the group co-operate, pick up cues, etc.?

Technical elements: How effective was the play in performance? Which scenes were powerful on stage? Which techniques worked well? Comment on lighting, sound and music.

The audience response: How did the audience respond?

What have you learnt from this experience and how will it help you in future devised projects?

> Always make reference to specific scenes to illustrate a point.
>
> **STUDY HINT**

THE BARE BONES

➤ The Edexcel exam requires candidates to submit a portfolio for Unit 1 (an exploration of different types of drama texts) and Unit 2 (an exploration of a published play).

➤ Each portfolio should consist of a maximum of six sheets of A4 paper and be between 1500–3000 words.

➤ The portfolio must consist of three sections.

Presenting the portfolio

Your portfolio might simply consist of continuous prose covering six sides of A4 (two sides for each section).

Remember though that drama is a visual and active art form. Your portfolio might usefully reflect that.

Successful portfolios not only have good content, which explains and demonstrates a candidate's knowledge, understanding and creativity, but they are also:

- attractively laid out
- accurately written
- interesting to read and look at.

Many candidates choose to present each section on one sheet of A3 paper or card set out as a poster containing:

- annotated photographs and sketches
- annotated extracts of scripts
- storyboards
- designs (these can be done on sheets of acetate that are overlain one upon the other to show the design at different stages)
- swatches of fabric
- examples of sound or lighting cues sheets.

The writing in a portfolio may be handwritten or word-processed. You may use a computer to assist in the design. The important thing is that your teacher must be able to state that you have done the work yourself.

The response phase

This part of the portfolio gives details of the different strategies used to understand the different **drama texts** (Unit 1) or **play** (Unit 2).

The section should:

- give a **brief** description of the texts or play being explored
- state which explorative strategies you used to develop your understanding
- say why you chose these strategies and how they helped develop your understanding.

A **drama text** is anything that might be used as a starting point for dramatic exploration. The text might be:

- a poem
- an object
- a piece of music
- an extract from a play script
- a piece of live theatre

- an extract from a film or television programme
- a newspaper or magazine article
- an extract from a novel or piece of non-fiction

Create a chart like this to make brief notes on which explorative strategies you used, why and the result.

Explorative strategy	Why did we use it?	What did we find out?
Still image		
Thought-tracking		
Narrating		
Hot-seating		
Role play		
Cross-cutting		
Forum theatre		
Marking the moment		
?		
?		

A picture speaks a thousand words! Annotated photographs can be used very effectively to show you and your group at work. Using a digital camera will allow you to alter the size of the images to suit your presentation and you can add speech balloons and thought bubbles to the images electronically.

You need to demonstrate that you know and understand the context of what you have been working on. Most importantly, you need to say:

- what the starting point meant to you and how, through drama, your understanding of that context has developed
- how your practical work and response has been influenced by what you know and understand about drama.

STUDY HINT

The development phase

In this section, you need to show:

- How your exploration of the texts or play developed through the use of the **drama medium** and the **elements of drama**.

- The script that has emerged from your work on the drama texts or play.

- Your understanding and interpretation of a scene or section of the play you have been working on.

The **drama medium** involves the purposeful use of the following to convey meaning to an audience:

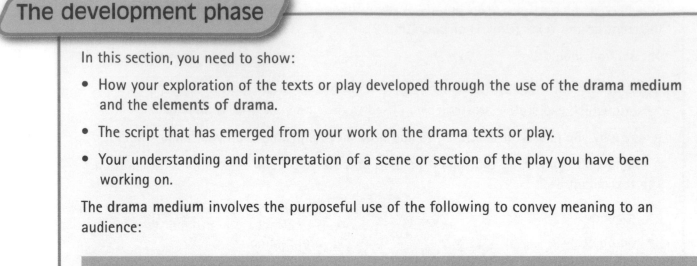

- costume, masks and make-up
- sound effects and music
- lighting
- space and levels

- set and props
- movement, mime and gesture
- voice
- spoken language

Create a chart like this to make brief notes on which **elements of drama** you focused on when developing your drama, as well as how and why.

Element of drama	How and why did we focus on this?
Action, plot and content	
Forms	
Climax and anti-climax	
Rhythm, pace and tempo	
Contrasts	
Characterisation	
Conventions	
Symbols	

The evaluative phase

In this section, you will reflect on what you have created and learnt through your **practical work**. As well as critically evaluating your own contributions and performance, you should say what other people in your group achieved. In this section, you should also show a knowledge and understanding of the social, cultural and historical context of the drama texts or play you have been working on and how this has influenced your work.

Use a chart like this to make brief evaluative notes:

Self-evaluation	What contribution did you make?	
	What special responsibilities did you have?	
	How well do you think you performed your tasks?	
	What was the most satisfying part of the project for you?	
	Were you disappointed with yourself for some reason?	
	What did you learn about yourself?	
	What else did you learn?	
Group evaluation	How well did other members of your group do in the project?	
	What impressed you in particular about their contribution?	
	How well did you work as a team?	
	Were there difficulties working together? How did you overcome them?	
	What did you learn about each other?	

Question

Billy Liar by Keith Waterhouse, selected scene: Act 1

From: ALICE goes out into the hall and puts on a coat that is hanging on the rack...
To: FLORENCE crosses the room and disappears up the stairs into the bedroom.

Discuss, in detail, how you would play either Billy or Florence in the selected scene. You will need to refer to voice, movement, gesture and facial expression, as well as to show how your chosen character responds to others on stage.

Answer

In Act 1 of Billy Liar by Keith Waterhouse, edition XX, from 'ALICE goes out into the hall and puts on a coat which is hanging on the rack... ' to 'FLORENCE crosses the room and disappears up the stairs into the bedroom' the role of Billy is a key one.[1] The start of this scene is basically Geoffrey telling Billy off, yet it would have to be shown that Billy wasn't particularly bothered. This can be achieved by the actor standing with his hands in his pockets, slumping maybe. Eye contact with Geoffrey would be minimal to show that he wasn't really listening. Billy could also gaze around or fidget with his hands. Occasionally nodding his head in acknowledgement of what his father was saying.[2]

As Billy walks into the kitchen, I feel he should have a slow and shuffling walk, as if he has just woken up, and is in no hurry to get to anywhere. Once Alice and Geoffrey leave and Billy is left alone with his grandmother, Florence, I feel that there should be far more silences, with Billy's eyes wandering, as if looking for something to do. 'I can't eat that egg. It's stone cold.' This should be said with a slightly whinging and disappointed tone, to display the fact that Billy is slightly immature. Yet when Florence starts her speech on how 'There's too much waste in this house... ' the actor playing Billy should sink back into his chair, possibly roll his eyes and give sarcastic nods and smiles at intervals and a long sigh from him when she finishes.[3]

'BILLY drinks and grimaces'. Here the actor should look, not at Florence, but maybe at his own cup of tea, possibly searching for a new conversation to bring up as opposed to sitting and listening to Florence's views on food waste.

A terribly important part of the scene is where both characters begin to go off into their own dream worlds.[4] At this stage it must be shown that Billy is starting to drift off as he says 'Sitting in a coffee bar... ' the actor would possibly begin to gaze, with eyes slowly glazing over as the character sinks deeper into his fantasy. Where the full stops are in his sentences, there must be rather long pauses in speech, to show him contemplating which direction the day dream will go in. 'Espresso with a girl. Duffel coat and dirty toe nails.'

The actor could possibly put his arm around Florence, showing Billy is so deeply engrossed in his fantasy that he sees his grandmother as the imaginary girl. Yet whilst Florence is still wittering on about life when she was young, Billy's face would still be facing forwards, still gazing, maybe pretending to listen to the troubles of the suicidal girl. 'I discovered her the night before, contemplating suicide.' Billy would now be sat upright in his chair, and leaning forwards to get closer to this imaginary girl. He could nod and give empathetic smiles as he tries to comfort her, 'less than a week ago my father felt the same as you. Suicidal.' His tone of voice would be gentle and slightly regretful, with a slight, small, 'brave' smile on his face.[5]

'Well, he'll never be world champion now. A broken man on two tin legs.'[6] Billy should now stand up, shaking his head at the tragic nature of his day dream, looking at the ground, and then start to limp, groaning and leaning against furniture with an anguished look on his face, biting his lip at trying to ignore his imaginary pain. Then as Florence says 'He's not right in the head.' Billy should suddenly become sheepish as he knows he is being watched. Standing up straight, no longer leaning on the furniture, and then start to rub his leg. As he offers the explanation of 'cramp', his eyes would be on his legs, refusing to meet Florence's stare.[7]

A slight expression of relief should spread across Billy's face as the doorbell goes, as it offers him a release from the awkward situation building with Florence, and so he should rush to answer it. As Arthur and Billy do their 'routine' it should all be terribly over-acted, with large gestures, such as Billy stamping his foot firmly on the ground and making a slight punching gesture in the air as he says 'They'll stand for him and lump it'. As he says 'Into the house Ned and bar the door!' he should almost shout and point wildly into his own house with a look of mock urgency on his face.[8]

The actor should double over clutching his stomach as the pair 'dissolve into laughter'. As they return inside, Billy should completely ignore the random comments made by Florence. He should once again be relaxed with a shuffling lazy walk going slowly back into the kitchen to finish his tea. 'Isn't it my Saturday off?' said with confusion and a furrowed brow as he sips his tea, slowly. Possibly with a slight guilty expression as well, to see his friend angry at him. His voice would be smaller and weaker than before, where he displayed such non-caring and idiocy.

As Florence gets up to leave, Billy could risk a cheeky sticking out of the tongue at her behind her back before turning once again to face Arthur at the end of the scene section.

Commentary on the answer

1 Specifies play and edition.

2 Explains what Billy is feeling – 'not bothered' – and how the actor can show this.

3 Explains how the actor could move and use his voice and gives specific references to the text.

4 Recognises that at this point in the scene a change in mood occurs and this must be reflected in the actions.

5 A good example of referencing voice and movement and relationship with other characters.

6 Recognises the point at which the tension changes as humour is injected and shows how the actor can interpret this.

7 Illustrates the relationship to another character.

8 Again, an example of physical interpretation of the text.

A sound discussion with detailed justification of how the role of Billy can be realised on stage.

THE BARE BONES

➤ This specimen answer is based on Section B of the WJEC written paper.

➤ You will be asked to write a piece of dialogue in play form, based on events within the play.

Question

A View From the Bridge by Arthur Miller

Imagine that Catherine and Rodolfo are walking home after being at the cinema on their first date. Write the dialogue for this scene in play form.

In your answer you **must** include:

- a description of where the scene takes place (You should include a suitable acting area, a suitable set, position of set and create an atmosphere. Remember your scene must be suitable for stage not for television!) *(4 marks)*

- effective stage directions (You should include an least one vocal and one movement direction, a pause and one that deals with an emotion.) *(4 marks)*

- an understanding of characters (based on your knowledge from the set text) *(4 marks)*

- references to events within the play (at least four references) *(4 marks)*

- other ideas you might have (You could be awarded marks for lighting directions, structure of your play, effective use of dialogue, etc.) *(4 marks)*

Answer   Commentary

The following answer is worth 20 marks. You can see from the bracketed annotations where the student's answer has been awarded marks.

The scene is set on a proscenium arch stage. (use of acting area) The stage is set up as a long pavement, grey and dirty with fire hydrants at intervals. There is a metal bench centre stage. The backdrop shows Brooklyn harbour and Brooklyn bridge, and in the distance, the New York skyline with its twinkling lights. (set and position) In the background, there are the faint noises of doors slamming and people arguing, as well as the waves lapping and a distant foghorn. Lighting is used to create the effect of street lamps and the full moon creates pools of light on the pavement. Dry ice could be used to create a foggy effect. (atmosphere)

There are exits stage right and stage left. Catherine and Rodolfo enter from stage left arm in arm. Rodolfo is singing one of the songs from the film. (understanding of character)

RODOLFO: 'Paper Doll' used to be my favourite song (reference to text) but now its 'New York, New York.'

He begins to sing again and with a surge of energy breaks away from Catherine and swings around one of the lamp posts. (movement direction)

CATHERINE: (with the sound of laughter in her voice) (vocal direction) Rodolfo, you are crazy! Do you want to be picked up by the cops? I don't think Eddie would be too happy if we arrived home in a cop car! (understanding of character)

They walk in a comfortable silence. (stage direction)

RODOLFO: (thoughtfully) Brooklyn is so different from Italy. (reference to text)

CATHERINE: (shyly) (stage direction referring to an emotion) Is it different in a good or bad way?

RODOLFO: You don't have fountains... (pause) but you have fire hydrants! You don't have orange and lemon trees but... (reference to text)

CATHERINE: (cutting in) ...but we have hot dogs!

They both laugh. Rodolfo takes her hand and leads her to the bench.

As she sits down there is a voiceover which acts as the voice of Eddie in her head. The words echo around her head, 'I think your skirt is too short' and she self-consciously tries to pull it down. (other idea) There is an awkward pause.

RODOLFO: (after a while) Catherine, why are you so afraid of what Eddie thinks? (reference to text)

CATHERINE: (defensively) Eddie has been like a father to me! He cares for me and I like to please him. He's a good man, Rodolfo. (understanding of character)

RODOLFO: (gently) I know he's a good man. I bless him but he doesn't like me... (pause) perhaps he's afraid I'll hurt his little doll. (understanding of character)

He looks at Catherine and very softly hums 'Paper Doll'. He leans across to kiss her but the mood is broken by the laughter of Louis and Mike who are walking home from a bar. They shout 'Goodnight Blondie'. (other idea)

RODOLFO: (laughs and shouts back) Come on, Catherine. Let us dance home as if we were the stars in the movies. (He grabs her hand and they dance offstage their laughter can be heard in the distance.) (other idea)

ALFIERI: (walks on and stares into the distance after them, quietly speaks almost to himself) And my practice is entirely unromantic...

The song 'Paper Doll' underscores his words. The lights fade slowly to a blackout. (other idea)

> **STUDY HINT**
> Use terms like naturalistic, minimalistic, expressionistic, etc. to describe the style of your set.

Question

Choose a production you have seen during your course that you considered successful.

Discuss, in detail, the contribution of one performer to the success of the production. You will need to give details of at least one particular scene or section and include reference to voice, movement, characterisation and relationships between characters on stage.

Answer

I thought the musical 'Blood Brothers' by Willie Russell was successful. I saw it at the Adelphi Theatre in London. The character who I thought added specifically to this success was Mickey.[1] This was because as the character changed and grew, so did the actor and his behaviour, which portrayed the character very well.[2]

Firstly the actor playing Mickey was a full-grown man, and so he had to exaggerate and emphasise his actions a lot, to give the audience the impression of a child. He used a high-pitched voice and spoke very fast and excitedly. The character is very outlandish and energetic, so the actor used most of the stage space, by making his movements large and 'over the top'.[3] For instance, when Mickey is pretending to drive a car, the actor jumped onto the floor, and thrust his arms and legs out in front of him, as though he were gripping a steering wheel. As he veers left and right the actor leans violently all the way over to one side or another. He makes loud car noises that differ according to his actions, and as he 'stops' he screeches loudly, leans all the way back, springs up, and bumps across the stage. His eyes are wide and he smiles with his teeth biting his lower lip to show his excitement.[4]

Another example of the actor portraying a child well is when Mickey pretends to ride a horse. The actor really does act as though he believed that there was an invisible horse. When mounting or dismounting it the actor swings his leg round in the air, he 'ties it up', pretends to pat and stroke it, and 'talks' to it, just as a child would if he was playing. He gallops around the stage making horse noises and imitates pulling the reins tightly to stop it. The audience find this effective because the actor is apparently playing, and illustrating the kind of innocent games that children play to express their vivid imaginations.[5]

The actor's interaction with Eddie is also very realistic.[6] Mickey wants to impress Eddie so he starts being naughty to show off. When the actor playing Mickey pretends to spit he leans really far back and then throws himself forward, as if he were making a tremendous effort. Afterwards, he sways back and forth on his heels beaming and looking really pleased with himself.

As the play progresses, so do the characters, and as they age time-wise, so the actors have to, visually, for the audience. Mickey reaches puberty, and as a teenager he has hit an awkward stage in his life.[7] The actor spends no time on the floor now, his stature changes to show an increase in maturity. When Mickey boasts to Eddie, the actor puffs out his chest and talks boldly in a loud, confident voice, but as soon as Linda comes along, he stops in his tracks. His stature shrinks a little, he stuffs his hands in his pockets and bows his head. Because he becomes worried about embarrassment, the actor pauses before talking to Linda, he makes no eye contact and stares at the ground instead and scuffs his feet so as to detract from what he's saying. He appears more nervous and less forward. The audience think this is funny and sympathises with him because many of them have experienced this themselves. When Mickey finishes talking to Linda the actor runs away laughing with Eddie to mask his embarrassment.

Again the play moves on. Mickey has just got out of prison and his attitude completely changes; the character becomes someone else. His stature reverts back down because the actor slumps his shoulders, he leans on walls for support because the actor has become weak. His speech becomes slow and minimal, his expression is constantly angry and dark, he screws up his face and constantly stares at the floor, his expression doesn't ever relax or change, he shuffles rather than walks and he looks completely dull and lifeless. He no longer raises his head to talk to anyone and makes no eye contact. This makes him seem cold and heartless and the audience's opinion of him completely changes. The actor appears to be unfriendly and aggressive. He occasionally loses his temper and explodes in a fury, he goes red, begins to shout and throw his arms into the air, and he remains in one place, but this stops abruptly and he sinks back into the shell of an empty, walking man. He seems miserable and spaced out, his eyes don't seem to move and the audience feels sorry for him because his life seems so hopeless, but the actor also makes the audience feel dislike as well now for the character because he shuts his family out and treats them so badly.[8]

This is why I feel that the actor playing Mickey was so effective in making the production successful, because he made it so plainly obvious to the audience how the character felt, there was visual evidence that one can comprehend and relate to which made the perception and understanding of the play all the easier.

Commentary on the answer

1 States that the production was successful and identifies the chosen character thus answering the question.

2 Distinguishes between actor and character.

3 Refers to vocal and movement skills and the impression they create.

4 Gives an example of what the actor did on stage.

5 Gives an example of the actor's movements and references the audience response.

6 Reference to a specific moment.

7 Refers to the actor's physical movements and use of voice and their relevance to the plot as time passes.

Don't just describe – analyse.

STUDY HINT

8 Explains how the actor interprets his changed circumstances through his movement and speech and the effect these have on the audience.

This is a sound and competent discussion with constant reference to audience response and specific moments.

Question

Choose a production you have seen during your course in which you felt design helped to create a strong effect on you as a member of the audience.

Discuss, in detail, at least one scene or section in which the design elements had a strong effect on you.

Answer

I found 'The Woman in Black' by Stephen Mallatrat adapted from the novel by Susan Hill, which I saw at The Fortune Theatre in London, to be a very frightening play.[1] As there are only two actors it needs a lot of design to keep the production not only interesting but also effective.[2]

In one section, 'The Actor' playing the character of Arthur Kipps is visiting the house of a lady who died, in order to take care of her possessions. Apart from a dog he is completely alone in the house. After a long day sorting through the lady's papers he tries to go to sleep, but he is laying down for about 20 to 30 seconds when he hears the sound of what seems to be a heartbeat. Arthur Kipps wakes up and the noise stops, but when he lies down it starts again. He goes to investigate and comes to a door that had never been opened before. As he approaches the door the noise becomes louder. Suddenly, we hear a blood-curdling scream, the 'heartbeat' stops abruptly and the lights go out. A gauze is used in the production and, as the lights come up behind the gauze we see that there is a bedroom behind it. We can now see that the noise was not a heartbeat but the sound of a rocking chair moving with no-one in it. I found this particular section very effective and successful. It required very accurate timing to create the correct effect.[3]

The gauze is a very effective part of the staging as it allows the scene to be changed without the audience being aware. In the previous scene the area behind the gauze represented a graveyard and the gauze gave it a foggy and very eerie effect.

When the gauze is lit from behind the audience can see the area of stage behind, but if it is only lit from the front then the audience cannot see behind it. This allows the action to continue while the scene behind the gauze is changed and this can be used very effectively. In this production the gauze was also used as a screen for projections. In the church scene of the funeral of Mrs Drablow a large crucifix was projected onto the screen and whenever 'The Actor' or Arthur Kripps approached Eel March House a projection of the house appeared on the gauze.[4]

The production used only a minimum of props and costumes. Sometimes only a jacket and a hat were used to distinguish two characters. Other props were made to represent several things. A wicker basket was used as the pony and trap, the seat on the train, a desk and a bed. There was a clothes rail stage right that allowed the actors to change easily between their characters without having to leave the stage.[5]

Sound effects were used effectively throughout the performance to build the scenes. Crows cawed in the background at the funeral scene, there was a howling wind on the foggy night and seagulls were heard outside when they were near Eel Marsh House as it was near the sea.[6] The music box which was used in Act 2 was very eerie. When Arthur Kripps first went into the child's bedroom he played with the music box but later on, we heard a scream and the stage went completely black. The audience was silent, and then we heard the sound of a music box and Arthur Kripps re-entered the room to find it trashed and the rocking chair moving by itself.[7]

Overall I think that the lighting, sound effects, minimal props and costumes made 'The Woman in Black' very effective. The timing of light and sound was perfect and evoked the full response from the audience. I saw the play a second time at the New Victoria Theatre in Woking but it did not have the same effect on me because I knew when certain 'frightening' things were about to happen.[8]

Commentary on the answer

1 States where the production was seen.

2 Provides the context for the need for 'a lot of design'.

3 A vivid description of the 'heartbeat' scene in Eel Marsh House. Good awareness of the need for timing but this point could be developed more.

4 Addresses the way in which the gauze is used and how it allows the scene to be changed without the audience knowing. Explains how the gauze works with lighting.

5 Mentions the minimal props and costumes but you could consider developing the reason why these are used – that this is a lawyer seeking the assistance of an actor to tell his story, using the facilities at hand in a closed theatre.

6 Mentions the use of sound effects but you could mention how they were used and what effect they created for the audience.

7 Good reference to the music box but the point could be developed – why was the music box so eerie? What feelings did it evoke and why?

8 A reasonably neat summary but more precision on the effects created would have improved the answer. The reference to seeing the production again is interesting but it could be developed into a useful point about the effects of surprise and the creation of tension.

THE BARE BONES

> ➤ The review of a live performance is an important part of your coursework.
> ➤ A review, which fulfils the required criteria, can give you 15% towards your final grade.
> ➤ Reviews should be up to 1500 words in length.

Introduction

The introduction of your review should include:

• What play did you see, where and when was it performed?

• Who performed it?

• The historical and cultural background to the play and a brief synopsis of the plot.

Main body

STUDY HINT

Always make reference to a specific scene to illustrate the point.

For example: 'At the start of the play, Mr Craven entered dressed in a black suit to symbolise that he was in mourning after his wife had died. The colour of his clothes also showed he was a very serious character.'

1 The performance of the actors:

• Did the actors identify with the characters?

• How did they use voice/pauses as part of their character?

• How did they use movement, facial expressions and gesture as part of the character?

• How did they interact on stage?

2 The technical aspects:

• What type of acting area was used? Why do you think that particular area was chosen?

• What was the style of the production? Naturalistic or symbolic?

• What was the scenic design? Did it reflect the themes of the play?

• What effect was achieved with lighting and sound?

• How did costume, make-up and hair help to develop the characters?

3 The messages of the play:

• What were the key messages of the play? How were these communicated to the audience?

• What did the director seem to want to achieve?

• How did the audience react?

Conclusion

The conclusion of your essay should deal with:

- What was your personal reaction to the performance?
- Did you enjoy it?
- What elements did it contain that appealed to you?
- Which particular scenes did you enjoy?
- Would you recommend the performance to other people?

Remember

1 Make comparisons with other productions you might have seen.

For example: 'The two Shakespearean productions I saw were completely different. 'Romeo and Juliet' was a modern interpretation, staged in the round and the two gangs were dressed in jeans and t-shirts. 'Twelfth Night' was set in Elizabethan times and was presented on a thrust stage.

2 Include visual evidence, e.g. diagrams of costume and set designs.

3 Use theatrical terminology where appropriate.

WJEC: practice questions

THE BARE BONES

➤ The WJEC exam paper is divided into two sections.
➤ You must answer questions on two plays.

Exam structure

Section A will ask questions on a specific section of the play. You will need to spend 35 minutes on this section. The questions in this section are structured and by following the guidelines on the paper you can achieve maximum marks.

In Section B you will be given a choice of questions. A dialogue question will always be given as one choice. The other question could be based on character or theme from the play. You are advised to spend 25 minutes on this section.

Question 1

Look at Act 2 of 'Spring and Port Wine': 'Everyone looks at Wilfred. Rafe opens the back door, goes outside, then returns holding the tray of herring. He takes it through into the living room.' to 'He swoons'.

Question 1 can follow two different formats. Format A will ask you who a character is and what their relationship is to another character. Format B will ask you who a character is and ask you to give some acting advice to the actor playing that part.

Answer for format A: *Who is Rafe? What is his relationship to Wilfred?*

Rafe is the strict and controlling father of the Compton household. Wilfred is his youngest son and in this scene he is in trouble because he has lied to his father over the disappearance of the herring.

Answer for format B: *Who is Rafe? How would he enter the living room?*

Rafe is the strict controlling father of the Compton household. When he enters the room the actor playing the role would stand very erect, enter slowly and look around the room slowly to show he is in control and that he will take his time to get to the truth. He would hold the plate of herrings out in front of him to start to make the family feel guilty and uneasy.

This question is worth 2 marks so you don't need to give a huge amount of information but you do need to be specific. 'Rafe is a man in the play.' is too general and doesn't give any information. Always relate relationship and acting details to the specified scene.

Q1 Deepen your thinking

Now try these other examples.

'Walking With Shadows':
Who is Lorna? What is her relationship to Jamie?

'As You Like It':
Who is Rosalind? What is her relationship to Duke Frederick?

Question 2

Question 2 will ask you to describe the moods of a particular character within the specified section.

This question is worth 3 marks and you must give three different moods to be awarded full marks. For example:
Describe Florence's mood at the beginning of 'Spring and Port Wine'.

Answer

Florence is extremely efficient and businesslike as she sorts out her mother's finances. She shows irritation and annoyance at her mother's haphazard system. She is shocked when her mother admits she lies to make the books balance.

Q2 Deepen your thinking

Now try these other examples.

'A View From the Bridge':
Describe Alfieri's different moods in his opening speech.

'Be My Baby':
Describe the Matron's mood in scene 2.

Question 3

Question 3 will ask you to describe a suitable costume for a character in the specified period. This question is worth 6 marks.

You must cover the following points to gain maximum marks:

• a specified period **relevant** to the play

• the colour and garments

• two reasons for your choice, e.g. what does it tell the audience about the character?

• hair and make-up.

Q3 Deepen your thinking

Describe suitable costumes for the following characters.

'Walking With Shadows':
The Shadow Chorus

'Be My Baby':
Mrs Adams in scene 2

Question 4

Question 4 will ask you how to direct a character within the specified scene. This question is worth 9 marks.

You must include:

• at least two reasons describing character motivation

• at least three vocal directions

• at least four directions referring to movement, gesture and facial expressions.

Q4 Deepen your thinking

Now try these other examples.

As a director what advice would you give to the actor playing the part of...

Catherine in the opening scene of 'A View From the Bridge'?

Celia in Act 1, scene 2 of 'As You Like It'?

AQA: practice questions

THE BARE BONES

The AQA examination paper is in two sections:
➤ Section A – Set texts
➤ Section B – Response to live productions

Set texts

In Section A, you will be given a selected scene or scenes and then an either/or question based on the selected scene(s). There will be one question on each of the set texts.

> **STUDY HINT**
>
> Make close reference to the specified scene(s).

For example:

EITHER:

Discuss, in detail, how you would play either _____ or _____ in the selected scene. You will need to refer to voice, movement, gesture and facial expression, as well as to how your chosen character responds to others on stage.

OR:

*Discuss, in detail, how **one** area of design might add to the overall effectiveness of the selected scene. In your answer you will need to show how your ideas relate to other aspects of design.*

Response to live productions

In Section B, there will be four questions, one on **performance**, one on **acting or design**, one on **design** and one on **emotional / audience response**.

The wording may be slightly different for each of the questions but if you look carefully you will see that the exam is asking for basically the same thing – it is only the emphasis that changes.

1 Performance questions

*Choose a scene or section from a production you have seen during your course. Discuss, in detail, what you felt to be **either** the strongest **or** the weakest performance by **one** actor and explain the reasons for the strengths or weaknesses. You will need to give details of a particular scene or section. You may wish to include reference to voice, movement, characterisation and relationships between characters on stage.*

*Choose a production you have seen during your course that you considered successful. Discuss, in detail, the contribution of **one** performer to the success of the production. You will need to give details of at least one particular scene or section and include reference to voice, movement, characterisation and relationships between characters on stage.*

2 Acting or design questions

*Choose a production you have seen during your course in which the acting or the design added to your enjoyment. Discuss, in detail, the ways in which **either** the acting **or** the design made the production enjoyable. You will need to refer to at least one particular scene or section that you found especially effective.*

*Choose a production you have seen during your course in which the acting or the design surprised you. Discuss, in detail, how **either** the acting **or** the design contributed to the overall effectiveness of one scene or section and explain in what ways you found it surprising.*

3 Design questions

*Choose a production you have seen during your course in which design played an important part. Discuss, in detail, the strengths and/or weaknesses of **one** scene or section. You will need to give reasons to justify your answer. You will need to explain in what ways the design contributed to the production.*

Choose a production you have seen during your course in which you felt design helped to create a strong effect on you as a member of the audience. Discuss, in detail, at least one scene or section in which the design elements had a strong effect on you.

4 Emotional / audience response questions

Choose a production you have seen during your course that created a strong audience response. Discuss, in detail, the scene or section that made the strongest impression and explain how the effect on the audience was created.

Choose a production you have seen during your course that you would recommend to others. Discuss, in detail, at least one scene or section that would justify your recommendation.

Quick quizzes

Who did what and when?

The origins of theatre

1 A _____ explores themes of death, power and justice.

2 Saying that someone is a 'Thespian' means that they are an _____ .

3 _____ was a well-known writer of Roman comedies.

4 Mystery plays were staged on moveable _____ _____ .

5 *Commedia dell'arte* troupes developed ideas for different scenes from brief descriptions of the action called _____ .

The theatre explosion

1 'The Theatre' was built in London in 1576 by _____ _____ .

2 Queen _____ was on the thrown when Shakespeare started writing his plays.

3 The first women actors appeared on stage in England during the reign of _____ ____

4 Melodrama was a popular form of entertainment in _____ Britain.

5 Melodramas relied on fast action and _____ to entertain the audience.

Theatre in the modern world

1 Naturalism attempted to show _____ _____ on stage.

2 Bertolt Brecht was a _____ from _____ .

3 'The Method' was a system of acting that was built on some of the ideas of the Russian director _____ _____ .

4 Samuel Beckett's plays are sometimes regarded as examples of the _____ of the _____ .

5 Some of the new British writers of the 1950s were referred to as the _____ _____ _____ .

The origins of theatre
1 tragedy 2 actor 3 Plautus 4 pageant wagons 5 scenario
The theatre explosion
1 James Burbage 2 Elizabeth I 3 Charles II 4 Victorian 5 sentimentality
Theatre in the modern world
1 real life 2 playwright, Germany 3 Konstantin Stanislavski 4 Theatre of the absurd 5 Angry Young Men

The language of drama

Match the key term to the definition in the boxes on the following page, e.g. 1 tableau = 7 A group of actors standing in a still image.

The answers are at the bottom of p 95.

Key term		Definition	
1	tableau	1	sound effects
2	thought-tracking	2	a type of drama in which the characters are played as if they were real people in a real world
3	narration	3	the 'type' or family that a drama belongs to
4	cyclorama	4	a line made up by an actor which isn't in the script
5	forum theatre	5	the part taken by an actor
6	plot	6	the term used when something is going on beneath what the characters are actually saying
7	FX	7	a group of actors standing in a still image
8	climax	8	the movement made by an actor which has a particular meaning
9	ensemble	9	a technique used by actors to build a character by thinking of one part of their body
10	genre	10	a form of theatre in which the audience is actively involved in shaping or reshaping a scene
11	style	11	the lines spoken by a number of different characters to each other
12	ad lib	12	the term for a group of actors who work closely together

13	characterisation	13	the unfolding events of a story
14	monologue	14	the moment of greatest tension
15	dialogue	15	the word used for when something stands for something else
16	melodrama	16	when a character speaks aloud what they are thinking at a given moment
17	centring	17	a remark made by a character directly to the audience
18	naturalism	18	the particular way in which something is done
19	symbol	19	a technique for telling a part of a story to the audience directly
20	sub-text	20	the way an actor uses voice, movement and gesture to show what they are like in a role
21	gesture	21	a speech made by just one character
22	aside	22	the back wall of the stage
23	proxemics	23	the word for objects used on stage
24	role	24	a term describing the way space is used to create meaning
25	props	25	a genre often associated with 'over-acting' by the characters

Key term	1	2	3	4	5	6	7	8	9	10	11	12	13
Definition	7												

Key term	14	15	16	17	18	19	20	21	22	23	24	25
Definition												

Answers to the language of drama:

Key term	1	2	3	4	5	6	7	8	9	10	11	12	13
Definition	7	16	19	22	10	13	1	14	12	3	18	4	20

Key term	14	15	16	17	18	19	20	21	22	23	24	25
Definition	21	11	25	9	2	15	6	8	17	24	5	23

Check your knowledge of different types of stage lanterns by filling in the chart below. Write in the name of each lantern and briefly describe what it is like and what it does.

Symbol	Name	Description

Lights

Key words

You may gain a few valuable **extra marks** by ensuring that you:

- use subject-specific vocabulary
- know what specialist terms mean
- spell them accurately.

Common spelling mistakes include:

amphitheatre (sometimes misspelled as 'amfitheatre')
centring (sometimes misspelled as 'centering')
character
chorus (sometimes misspelled as 'choros')
narration
proscenium
proxemics
rehearsal
scene (often misspelled as 'sence')
scenery (often misspelled as 'scenary')
soliloquy
tableau (singular) tableaux (plural – note it has an 'x', not an 's')
theatre (you might get away with the American spelling – 'theater' – but it is not ideal.)

Punctuation

Drama is a different subject from English but uses the same language – and the same rules! Sentences should start with capital letters and finish with full stops. Quotations should be set apart from your comments by using quotation marks.

The convention is to use capital letters for names of plays and playwrights. The name of the play should be put in quotation marks.

For example:

'A View From the Bridge' by Arthur Miller

'Blue Remembered Hills' by Dennis Potter

Dos and don'ts

Do:

- read the question carefully.

- make sure you know what you are being asked to do.

- plan your answer before you start writing.

- divide your answer into paragraphs. Put all your ideas about the same aspect into one paragraph.

- use the PQD (point, quote, develop) formula as far as possible.

    Make your **point**.

    Support what you are saying with a **quotation**.

    Develop your point further, paying attention to how things might be done.

- use annotated diagrams and sketches if they will help make your point clearer and refer to them in your written answer.

- analyse and justify.

Don't:

- waffle.

- imagine the examiner knows nothing about the play (so don't waste time re-telling the story in detail).

- imagine the examiner has exactly the same ideas about the play as you do (so don't forget to explain why you think what you do).

- use quotations without adding a comment about what they show.

- draw tiny diagrams and sketches and forget to explain what they are showing.

- make emotional judgements ('I thought it was great!') without explaining how you came to feel the way you do.

Questions will be about what plays might look and sound like when they are performed.

Content and form

Your discussions of drama should contain comments on both content and form and recognise that they are dependent on each other.

Content This refers to **what** is being said in the drama.

Make sure you recognise the difference between narrative and thematic content:

'The Crucible' tells the story of a group of villagers in seventeenth century America who are accused of witchcraft. It focuses in particular on the character of John Proctor who stands by his innocence but is nevertheless hanged at the end. The play explores the themes of honesty and justice and is critical about the way governments can misuse their power.

Form This refers to **how** it is being said. In drama things are 'said' not just through words but also through action, sound, light and design. You need to show an understanding of how the different elements of drama can be used to convey meaning:

At the end of 'The Crucible' Proctor's wife Elizabeth must look physically drained by the emotion, holding herself up by gripping the bars of the cell window. Even so, her voice could be full of pride. When she says, 'He has his goodness now. God forbid I take it from him!' the words could be delivered quite slowly and evenly and Elizabeth could make an obvious effort to hold her head up to show that she is still strong and calm inside.

As she speaks her last line a drum roll begins and builds to a threatening crescendo. It is violent and militaristic but, by contrast, the orange glow of the morning sun begins to light Elizabeth's face suggesting that she will be saved. Meanwhile the actor playing Hale should fall to his knees looking terrified and lost as he 'weeps in frantic prayer' suggesting that he knows he has done wrong and will suffer for it.

STUDY HINT

Drama is an art form. It tries to understand the world by looking at it in new ways. There is never just one right answer – your creative ideas about how a play might be staged and what it might mean will be valued.

Skills, techniques and genres

Preparation techniques

actor / designer objectives

breathing exercises

mantle of the expert

mirror exercises

movement exercises

Relaxation exercises

research

role on the wall

CHECK!

Do you know enough about these to be able to talk and write about them with confidence as well as use them in practice?

Performance skills (voice)

accent

addressing the audience

mannerism

pitch

strength / tension

tone

volume

Rehearsal techniques

blocking

character modelling

character objectives

emotional memory

forum theatre

hot-seating

internal dramatic dialogue

mime

off-text improvisation

on-text improvisation

role reversal

tableaux

thought-tracking

working in units

CHECK!

Have you used these in your practical work? Can you say why you used them and what effects they had on your work?

Performance skills (body)

circle of attention

facial expression

facing out of the drama

gesture

levels

mannerisms

movement

posture

strength / tension

Performance skills (timing)

- awareness of audience
- flow
- pace
- rhythm
- pause

CHECK!

When planning and reflecting on your practical work, have you taken account of these technical techniques?

Technical techniques

- drawing plans and diagrams
- identifying performance demands
- identifying textual demands
- knowing the performance space
- preparing cue-sheets
- recognising technical interdependence
- using equipment correctly and safely
- using materials successfully

Group techniques

- banners
- chorus
- counterpoint
- flash-back
- flash-forward
- monologue / solo
- narration
- physical theatre
- repetition and echo
- slow motion
- synchronised movement
- use of levels

Most popular genres

- comedy
- farce
- horror
- melodrama
- pantomime
- thriller
- tragedy

Other genres

- black comedy
- *Commedia dell 'arte*
- fantasy
- historical drama
- kitchen-sink drama
- light opera
- mime
- musical
- period drama
- poetic drama
- romance
- satire
- sci-fi
- soap opera
- theatre of the absurd
- tragi-comedy
- whodunnit / detective

CHECK!

Have you considered how your own work, or work you have seen, fits into the different families or 'genres' of drama?

Key figures in drama

Here are the names and a very few details of some of the figures whose work has been influential in the development of the theatre as we know it today.

Before the Common Era (BCE)	
Thespis (c. 534)	Thespis was the first dramatist to use an actor alongside the chorus.
Famous playwrights in Ancient Greece: • Aeschylus (525–456) • Euripides (480–406) • Sophocles (495–406) • Aristophanes (448–385)	
Aristotle (384–322)	Although Aristotle was not a dramatist himself, he drew up a set of 'rules' for drama that influenced writers for centuries afterwards.
Famous playwrights in Ancient Rome: • Plautus (254–184) • Terence (190–159)	
Common Era (CE)	
James Burbage (1530–1597)	Burbage built the first permanent theatre in London. It was simply called The Theatre. Its timbers were later used to build The Globe.
Famous playwrights in the time of Elizabeth I and James I: • Christopher Marlowe (1564–1593) • Ben Jonson (1572–1637) • William Shakespeare (1564–1616)	
Thomas Killigrew (1612–1683) and William D'Avenant (1606–1668)	Charles II awarded Killigrew and D'Avenant special licenses to perform plays. As a result, their theatre companies were the only ones allowed to perform 'legitimate plays', that is, plays without singing and dancing, for the next century.
Aphra Behn (1640–1689)	The best-known of a number of women playwrights at work during the reign of Charles II. Their work paved the way for later work by women dramatists.
Carlo Goldoni (1707–1793)	An Italian dramatist who drew on the earlier form of *Commedia dell'arte* and influenced the work of later writers of comedy and farce.
David Garrick (1717–1779)	The greatest actor of his time, Garrick's technique of playing characters as if they really existed was revolutionary.

Sir Henry Irving (1838–1905)	A great actor in the time of Queen Victoria and especially known for his declamatory (that is, 'big') acting style. Irving was the first actor to be knighted.
Dion Boucicault (1822–1890)	A leading writer and director of melodramas, Boucicault helped introduce the laws on copyrighting which stopped work produced by one writer simply being copied by others.
Henrik Ibsen (1828–1906) August Strindberg (1849–1912) Anton Chekhov (1860–1904)	Famous writers associated with naturalisim, a movement which tried to replace the big, over-the-top style of melodrama with something that looked and sounded more true to life.
Konstantin Stanislavski (1863–1938)	A great Russian director who tried to give the illusion of truth and reality in his work. He later influenced the American director Lee Strasberg who formulated what became known as 'the method', a way of training actors to 'become' the characters they were playing.
Edward Gordon Craig (1872–1966)	An influential designer whose ideas have helped shape many modern theatre productions.
Antonin Artaud (1896–1948)	A French actor, poet and director, Artaud was influenced by ritualistic forms of theatre. He strove for symbolism and spirituality. His writing has influenced modern writers and directors such as Steven Berkoff and Peter Brook.
Bertolt Brecht (1898–1956)	A German writer and director, Brecht tried to use theatre to get audiences to think about political and moral issues by rejecting illusion and mimicry.
Samuel Beckett (1906–1989)	Along with Eugene Ionesco and Jean Genet, Beckett is a writer whose work is often associated with the Theatre of the absurd which sees mankind's plight as essentially pointless.
Dennis Potter (1935–1994)	Dennis Potter is best known for his innovative work in television drama.
Arthur Miller (1915–2005)	Probably the greatest of American playwrights.

Do you know what these 60 words mean? Tick them if you do or look them up to remind yourself.

	Tick here if you know what the word means	Look at this page if you need reminding
absurd		16
accepting		22
ad lib		22
amphitheatre		27
antagonist		24
anti-hero		24
aside		23
auditorium		20
barndoor		33
blocking		23
centring		23
characterisation		23
chorus		24
climax		24
cross-cutting		28
cross-fade		35
cyclorama		20
dialogue		24
direct address		24
ensemble		93
epilogue		25
flashback		29
forum theatre		29
Fresnel		33
gel		34
genre		25
gobo		34

hubris		25
improvisation		23
iris		34
melodrama		13
metaphor		25
monologue		25
narration		30
naturalism		14
patch		35
pathetic fallacy		25
plot		25
preset		35
prologue		25
promenade		27
proscenium		27
protagonist		24
proxemics		23
rake		20
rigging		35
role		23
set		21
soliloquy		25
strobescope		33
style		94
stylisation		23
symbol		94
tableau		31
theatre-in-the-round		26
thespian		7
traverse		27
wings		21

http://www.theatremuseum.org.uk

The Theatre Museum is based in London. This site will tell you about their extensive collection of archive materials and objects, projects, exhibitions and how to use their facilities for your own research.

http://www.rsc.org.uk

There is a really helpful online guide to Shakespeare's plays on this site featuring synopses of the stories, character outlines, tips for directing, interviews with actors and some excellent production photographs.

http://www.thestage.co.uk

Use this site to find out what plays are being performed in your area and elsewhere. The site is also a useful source of reviews.

http://www.theatrenet.com

This site offers helpful links to different theatres and has a particularly useful news archive through which you can look up articles about plays, actors, directors, and so on.

http://www.shakespeares-globe.org

Take a virtual tour of Shakespeare's Globe Theatre on this site. There are loads of well-presented materials about Shakespeare, his plays and performances at The Globe.

http://www.doollee.com

This site boasts that it has notes on 13 000 modern playwrights and their plays. It is a useful quick reference guide.

http://www.bbc.co.uk/coventry/content/rich_media/shakespeare_game.shtml

This game is fun to play and will be a good piece of light-hearted revision for you.

http://www.bbc.co.uk/drama

This site gives details about current and recent television and radio drama productions.

http://www.ald.org.uk/gallery.php

ALD stands for the Association of Lighting Designers. Check out the Gallery on this site for some truly inspirational images of productions.

Notes

Notes

Notes

Notes

Notes